FROM LAID OFF TO
LIBERATED

FROM LAID OFF TO
LIBERATED

A Guide to Navigating Stress,
Grief, & Growth After Job Loss

AMY BLOUSTINE

FROM LAID OFF TO LIBERATED

A Guide to Navigating Stress, Grief, & Growth After Job Loss

Copyright © 2025 by Amy Bloustine

ISBN: 979-8-9941168-0-7
Library of Congress Control Number: 2025925752

For permission requests, email the publisher at:
Of The Day Press
ofthedaypress@gmail.com

Of The Day Press
Broomfield, Colorado

Printed in the United States of America
10 9 8 7 6 5 4 3 2 1

First Edition

CONTENTS

Preface

The Interviews   5

Chapter 1
When I Was Laid Off . . .   **7**

My Story   8

Chapter 2
Laid Off or Fired?   **15**

Interview with Ed: "Light at the End of the Tunnel"   16
Were You Laid Off, Fired, or Furloughed?   18
The Myriad of Reasons for Being Laid Off, Fired, or Furloughed   20
Revisiting Ed   23
Reader Engagement   25

Chapter 3
The Impact of Being Laid Off   **27**

Interview with Client A.: "Only You Know What's Best for You."   28
Not All Layoffs are Created Equally   34
The Expanded Impact   36
Revisiting Client A.   41
Reader Engagement   42

Chapter 4
The Three-State Recovery Process

45

Interview with Dianne: "Life Happens, What Do We Do With It?" 47
Rest and Recovery Are Essential   49
My Personal Experience with Rest and Recovery   53
Not Just for After a Layoff   54
Revisiting Dianne   59
Reader Engagement   61

Chapter 5
Can You Recognize Burnout in Yourself?

63

Interview with Natalie: "Advocate for Yourself." 65
Recognizing Burnout   71
Supporting Yourself and Others   72
Revisiting Natalie   76
Reader Engagement   78

Chapter 6
Your Transition and Transformation Journey

79

Interview with Client B.: "Where is the Choice In All This?" 80
Change Shapes Our Lives   83
Transitioning After Layoffs   85
Transformations You Might Not Have Expected   91
Navigating Your Transition and Transformation   93
Revisiting Client B.   94
Reader Engagement   96

Chapter 7
Introspection is The Greatest Gift To Yourself

99

Interview with Gina: "Embracing the Journey of Starting Over" 100
Introspection: What are You Waiting For?   104
The Value of Introspection   106
Lean in so You Can Move Forward   107
Revisiting Gina   111
Reader Engagement   113

Chapter 8
Are You Just Your Job?   **115**

Interview with Holly: "The Best Thing I Didn't Know I Wanted"   117
A Change in Identity   121
Prioritizing Yourself Over Your Job   123
Building Your Job Around Your Life   127
What to Do Next   129
Revisiting Holly   131
Reader Engagement   132

Chapter 9
"Laid Off" Aren't Bad Words   **133**

Interview with Bryant: "What's Broken and How To Fix It"   134
Changing the Conversation   137
What to Say and What Not to Say   139
Layoffs, the Compassionate Way   140
No Shame, No Guilt, and No Judgment   142
Revisiting Bryant   144
Reader Engagement   146

Chapter 10
Survivor's Guilt After Layoffs   **147**

Interview with Jeremy: "I Woke Up with a Smile"   149
You Survived a Layoff: Now What?   153
Impact of Layoffs on the Survivor   158
Impact of Layoffs on the Company   158
Revisiting Jeremy   160
Reader Engagement   162

Chapter 11
Mental Health In the Workplace and Beyond   **165**

Interview with Ellie: "We Need a Voice and a Platform"   168
Mental Health in the Workplace   171
What Mental Health in the Workplace Should Look Like   179
Shifting Awareness to Action   181
Revisiting Ellie   184
Reader Engagement   187
Additional Resources   188

Chapter 12
It Was the Best Gift, Just in the Ugliest Wrapping Paper 189

Conclusion

Appendices
Appendix 1: Connecting Everything   205

Early Conversations   206
When Should We Have the Talk ... About Being Laid Off or
Fired?   208

Appendix 2: Additional Interviews   215

Appendix 3: Reader Engagement Questions by Chapter 224

Acknowledgments

Endnotes

About the Author

PREFACE

"If you're on this call, you are part of the unlucky group that is being laid off," Vishal Garg said on the call.[1] This is how, in December 2021, Garg laid off nine hundred employees in a single Zoom call. Why Garg thought this was a good approach is baffling. When the story of his error in judgment hit the headlines, he unlocked a new set of fears for employees and the treatment they can expect from their employers.

Something has got to change.

By assessing the layoff landscape, we can chart a path forward that addresses the impact layoffs have on us as individuals, as a community, and as a culture. According to Zippia, in 2022, there were 15.4 million layoffs in the United States. Unfortunately, layoffs continued at drastic rates in 2023, and "Over 305,000 U.S. workers were laid off over the year in a series of mass layoffs that started most notably with tech companies, but then spread across industries."[2] Every day, we read headlines about ongoing layoffs across all industries, the tremendous impact on the individuals affected, and on the companies themselves. Logically, we understand this is a business transaction, but when someone says, "It's not personal; it's business," it doesn't mitigate the collateral damage it causes. It might not feel personal for the person conducting the layoffs, but it is incredibly personal for the individual being laid off; it should be personal, and that's okay.

During COVID, we understood why layoffs were conducted virtually. Still, it has been over five years since the pandemic began, and we need to improve how we communicate to someone that their role is no longer needed and that they are being laid off. Bringing a remote employee into the office just to let them know they've been laid off, especially in a public setting, isn't compassionate—it's cruel. As is a nine-hundred-person Zoom call layoff. Google wasn't much better—they notified employees via email, and some received the news in the middle of the night. And if you are one of the employees who has been laid off this way, it's not your fault and you are not alone.

Anyone who has been through a layoff knows its impact on them both personally and professionally. I was, myself, laid off in 2013. Honestly, it shook me to my core. And I've since worked with hundreds of clients undergoing a career transition—many cried and felt hopeless after being laid off, wondering how they would get through it. They often asked how others managed and how I navigated my own experience. I am frequently asked, "How did your other clients get through this? Is what I am feeling normal? Am I going to be okay?"

Writing a book was never something I imagined I would do. However, after seeing the trauma my clients have experienced, I realized that their stories of being laid off, as well as the resulting transitions and transformations, needed to be told. To manage expectations, let me be clear: this book is not about how to find a new job; rather, it focuses on the human side of what happens when someone is laid off—how their lives are impacted, how they navigate the experience, and what comes next. Most importantly, it focuses on sharing stories of hope.

I gave a lot of thought to how I wanted to tell these stories—how to capture the raw emotions of the journey someone goes through, but most importantly, to communicate that it's okay to talk about being laid off, to erase the shame, guilt, and stigma associated with it, and to create a safe space for people to discuss what happened to them without feeling judged. I interviewed individuals who have experienced layoffs, sometimes multiple times, and now I am sharing them with you. Hopefully, these stories will resonate and you will find a sense of calm and comfort in knowing that you will be okay; you will get through this and emerge stronger from the experience. I say this from both personal and professional experience.

Years ago, a client told me that being laid off was, "The best gift I got, just in the ugliest wrapping paper." I will never forget those words; they have stuck with me ever since, and I wholeheartedly believe them to be true. Being laid off was the best thing that happened to me, a true gift, and I am thankful every day for it. When we are in the moment, it is hard to acknowledge the possibility that it is a gift, but after the fog has lifted and you're ready to process this experience, it is amazing what can come from it.

I have been a certified life and career coach, as well as a trained recovery coach, since 2014. Additionally, I am a time management coach, a layoff coach, and a layoff consultant. I have worked with clients from diverse backgrounds and from a wide range of industries. My primary focus is on career and life coaching, where I assist clients in navigating career and organizational developments. I support clients in career transition due to layoffs, those who are currently employed and seeking new opportunities, and those aiming to advance in their careers. My firsthand experience and the journey alongside my clients enable me to understand what being laid off feels like from various perspectives, not just my own.

The impact of being laid off is devastating and life-changing. Whether we are the ones who have been laid off, those conducting the layoffs, or the survivors at a company after a layoff, we live with it every day. We need to eliminate the shame, guilt, and stigma associated with being laid off. The internal judgment that someone faces is so daunting that we have to—no, we must change the narrative around layoffs. We need to foster a different culture regarding how we talk about layoffs, process them, and move forward after them.

Being laid off is uncomfortable, but it is essential to delve into it and talk about it. To set the stage for the book, chapter one begins with my experience of being laid off, its impact on me both personally and professionally, and my transition and transformation journey. The topics and themes of each chapter were selected based on the interviews I conducted and the key takeaways that other clients have shared with me. We will explore the differences between being laid off, fired, and furloughed, the effects of layoffs, the three-state recovery process, how to identify burnout, your transition and transformation journey, the idea that introspection is the greatest gift you can give yourself, how to recognize that having a career-centric identity can be problematic, how to grapple with survivor's guilt after a layoff, the importance of mental health in the workplace and beyond, and, finally, I will wrap up with a story from my own life today and why being laid off, as my client said so many years ago, was the best gift, just in the ugliest wrapping paper.

Pure and simple, being laid off sucks and can be devastating, but it can also turn out to be a very good thing. I want everyone who reads this book to gain a better understanding of what it means to be laid off, to have a clearer picture of how to live life in a better way, and to recognize how you show up every day for yourself and those around you. These stories are for, by, and about those who have experienced being laid off.

THE INTERVIEWS

I can't proceed further without sharing what an amazing experience it has been to interview everyone featured in this book and to be a part of their journey. After hearing their stories, seeing and hearing their tears, I knew I had to write this book and share their experiences. However, I never anticipated the impact each story would have on me. It wasn't just about the stories but also about spending time with each person as they were vulnerable, laughed, cried, got angry, and had some "aha" moments. They allowed me to enter their space and participate in this transformative experience.

Many of the individuals I interviewed were clients, but I also spoke with others who were referred to me for the book or whom I knew through different channels. Regardless of how I knew them, I felt incredibly fortunate and honored that everyone allowed me to hold the space for them and trusted me. They showed their most authentic selves, fully transparent, and for many, the day of the interview marked the first time they'd discussed their experiences and relived what had happened to them. Many had not yet processed what had occurred or had the opportunity—or desire—to truly discuss their experiences in this way. I provided a platform for them to talk about being laid off without judgment or assumptions, and I know they all appreciated it.

Every story is unique, powerful, and filled with rich details and emotions. Although they share many of the same themes and connections, they are also quite different. I was deeply inspired by every interview I conducted, and I hope I have accurately captured every emotion, every thought-provoking moment, and every piece of advice and encouragement. These stories aren't just for those who have been laid off to connect with others who've had similar experiences; they also provide insight into what someone goes through and how others in their life are affected—families, friends, colleagues, and even the companies themselves.

This book is heartfelt and guides you step-by-step through the various realities of being laid off. I hope it is thought-provoking and helps you move forward with grace, kindness, and compassion. So many of us share the same identities, fears, emotions, vulnerabilities, hopes, and dreams. After reading this book, I hope you feel seen and heard.

CHAPTER 1

When I Was Laid Off . . .

It has been challenging to decide how to share my story with you. Should I discuss the details of where I worked, the toxic work environment, the people, the leadership, the culture, the work I wanted to do but wasn't doing, or the person I became while I was there? Or should I tell you that being laid off from my job was honestly the best thing that ever happened to me—the kick in the ass I needed? Thank goodness it happened when it did.

My story is just a small part of this journey; it's really more about all the other wonderful people you will read about—their experiences of being laid off, who they are, where they come from, and, most importantly, where they are now. The people I interviewed are extraordinary in their own ways, primarily because they shared their vulnerability. They were brave enough to express what being laid off felt like, how it changed their lives, and the gifts they unexpectedly received out of the experience. This holds true for me as well. So here is my story . . .

MY STORY

I loved my job working in the substance-abuse field. I worked with and learned from amazing people who became like family; they are still some of my closest friends today. So many talented individuals were part of that team. I was committed to the work which provided an excellent opportunity to grow, learn, and evolve in my career. Some people had been with the organization since it had begun, twenty-five years previously, and their long tenure must hold significant meaning. Our work mattered because the people we impacted needed our help, tools, and resources, and we were at the forefront of the field.

I have always been drawn to helping people which will always be a part of who I am. Working for this organization made a lot of sense, given my career path at the time. I navigated through the first four years easily, perhaps it was a honeymoon phase, but as the excitement faded, things began to shift in the last three and a half years. Of course, there is no perfect organization. Perfect does not exist—whether in a non-profit, for-profit, or whatever else.

In my case, personalities were changing, the work we were doing was shifting—not in a good way—and there were clear signs of significant problems. The organization's landscape was also evolving: the culture, our leadership, and our commitment to work seemed different. People were unhappy, and staff morale was at an all-time low.

For me, though, the most significant shift occurred within me. I often took work home at night, worked on weekends, and felt so tired and unhappy that I didn't want to be around people or go out and do things. I live in NYC, an amazing city, and I was letting life pass me by. I was hiding behind this job and making every excuse for how I was living my life. I remember looking at pictures of myself from my last job, and I looked so unhappy. I wasn't even trying to embrace this incredible city with wonderful friends and opportunities.

As time passed, I became someone I did not want to be. My colleagues and I started complaining about how awful things were and how much we disliked working there. As we all know, misery loves company. However, the ironic part was that, despite my discontent, I wasn't taking any steps to leave. I didn't try to find a new job or attempt to change my life. I was becoming the person I vowed I would never become. It's easy to get caught up in the conversation when we're all willing participants. We all had something in common, and at the end of the day, it was comforting to have people around me who understood my feelings. However, this can be a trap—caught in a routine that becomes increasingly negative.

We all become complacent at times; our lives settle into a routine, and why change that? The money was good. I woke up every day with somewhere to go; I saw my friends daily and felt a sense of purpose. However, I couldn't see what was right in front of me; I was hiding behind this job because I also didn't want to confront the real person in the mirror—myself. I knew I was unhappy, but that was acceptable for the moment because it felt better than the alternative. At least, that's what I kept telling myself.

Looking back, I knew the layoff was coming. We all sensed something was happening in the office. There were too many closed-door meetings, a strange vibe in the atmosphere, and people just weren't being themselves. I can now say with certainty that I felt deep down there would be layoffs, but I never thought it would happen to me, not really . . . Not even when I joked with my friends that I was probably the one who would be laid off, and then we laughed it off. When I started being excluded from emails and meetings, I convinced myself it was simply an oversight. I didn't want to see the truth.

I remember being at an offsite meeting at a local college with my boss and another colleague. There was a sign on the wall about a résumé writing class, and I joked that I should attend it or update my résumé. I should have realized something was wrong because neither of them laughed. The layoff occurred about a month later, and, of course, my boss knew what was happening so my joke didn't seem so funny to him at that moment . . . or maybe the joke was on me.

The day it happened felt surreal. I was so stressed at work that I'd developed stomach issues. I had been sick the night before, so I worked from home the next day. Early that morning, I emailed my boss and the head of HR to inform them that I was not feeling well and would be working from home. Around 10:00 a.m., my boss called and said, "You need to go into the office." I understood what those words meant. I immediately asked if I was being fired, and he replied, "I don't know, but you need to go into the office." I jumped into a cab for what felt like the longest ride of my life. When I arrived at the office, I threw my things on the desk, walked to the HR manager's office, and said to her, "So let's get this over with." She was clearly taken aback, and I learned later she was upset because I had "messed up her schedule for layoffs that day."

Our open-concept office where all the offices had glass walls, allowed everyone to see everything happening, even though a private conference room was available. We walked into the CEO's office and sat down. It was the CEO, the HR manager, and me. My boss wasn't there because he'd chosen not to come into the office that day. I later found out he knew exactly what was going on. He was one of the ones who'd decided to let me go and he'd been too afraid to say anything when he called me at home to go into the office.

The CEO and HR manager explained that my role had been eliminated due to a reorganization. I remember about 85 percent of the conversation. When you're told that you no longer have a job, you tend to stop listening, and everything comes to a halt and stops making sense at that point. But I will never forget this because it is the worst thing to say when laying someone off—they said, "It's not personal; it's just business." It may not be personal to them, but it was certainly personal to me, the person whose life had just undergone a significant change. Every bit of it was personal.

After this horrible conversation occurred and I regained my composure, the office had someone on-site to guide me through the outplacement package I would receive, and I packed up and left before lunch. As I left that day still in shock, I didn't know what to do with myself for the rest of the day. What would I tell people? How would I tell my family? What would people think of me? What's next? So many questions swirled through my head, yet I wasn't ready to answer them. I wasn't prepared for whatever that "next thing" was supposed to be.

I remember walking into the lobby of my apartment building and seeing some of my closest friends who lived there. I told them what had happened. They didn't know how to respond, and I didn't fault them for it. The funny thing is, when you tell someone that you've just been laid off, they often don't know how to react. What I've found is that people fear saying the wrong thing. I understand that sometimes people may not know how to help but staying away and remaining silent is not the answer. Just showing up for a friend or loved one makes a difference and helps in ways you can't imagine.

So what was next? Personally, I wanted to answer this question immediately. I was eager for my next chapter. Although I was uncertain about what it would look like, where it would lead me, or how I would get there, I knew it was out there, waiting to be discovered.

When something like this happens in our lives—a death, a divorce, a loss, a miscarriage, or whatever it might be—it involves learning to change, being open, engaging in introspection, and embracing vulnerability. It also serves as an excellent reminder of the importance of the people in our lives and how we may take these friendships for granted.

There is no doubt that if you are laid off, your world is turned upside down. Everything you know and everything you have worked so hard for changes, and it is not something you can control or decide for yourself. Although I knew I needed and wanted to leave that job, someone else took the power and control of that decision away from me. I struggled with that a lot. I wanted to make that decision for myself and control when and how I would leave. But that's not how things work out sometimes.

I also struggled with the cowardice exhibited by my boss—

he lacked the courage to come into the office that day, as my time there was coming to an end. He was involved in the decision to let me go but chose not to be there to tell me personally. For so many of us, it's not just the fact that we were laid off, it's more about how it occurred. Sometimes, you truly see someone's true colors and their real nature in these situations.

There is a powerful quote from a speech written by Theodore Roosevelt titled "Citizenship in a Republic," often referred to as "The Man in the Arena." Something incredibly impactful about this spoke to me and allowed me to explore, breathe, be present, and navigate this next phase of my life. I am only capturing the part that resonated most with me, but I encourage you to read the entire speech and delve further into its meaning. I am sure it will resonate differently for you than it did for me, but it is certainly worth the read.

> *"Vulnerability is not weakness, and the uncertainty, risk, and emotional exposure we face every day are not optional. Our only choice is a question of engagement. Our willingness to own and engage with our vulnerability determines the depth of our courage and the clarity of our purpose; the level to which we protect ourselves from being vulnerable is a measure of our fear and disconnection.*
> *"When we spend our lives waiting until we're perfect or bulletproof before we walk into the arena, we ultimately sacrifice relationships and opportunities that may not be recoverable,*

we squander our precious time, and we turn our backs on our gifts, those unique contributions that only we can make.

"Perfect and bulletproof are seductive, but they don't exist in the human experience. We must walk into the arena, whatever it may be—a new relationship, an important meeting, our creative process, or a difficult family conversation—with courage and the willingness to engage. Rather than sitting on the sidelines and hurling judgment and advice, we must dare to show up and let ourselves be seen. This is vulnerability. This is daring greatly."

Now you know how my journey began, setting me on a new and incredibly exciting path. I had many questions but no answers about what would happen next and how my life would unfold. I knew I would be okay and that everything would work out, but I didn't know when. I realized that to navigate this journey and gain clarity and understanding about my life, I first needed to be open, let things unfold as they should, and trust both the process and myself.

I am the type of person who needs to know what comes next. I need structure and to understand the reasons behind things. I had to learn to be comfortable with the uncomfortable and mostly trust myself, believing that whatever happens next occurs for a reason. I discovered how to draw from others' experiences, knowledge, and support, trusting that I would figure things out. I learned that I didn't have to do it alone and *shouldn't* do it alone.

You shouldn't, either.

CHAPTER 2

Laid Off or Fired?

D o you understand the difference between being laid off and being fired? They have distinct meanings. Understanding the differences will help you reconcile your feelings about your unique situation. The emotional impact between the two can be significant.

The interview with Ed, that you are about to read, taught me so much about how we perceive and interpret words differently. How the terms "laid off," "fired," and "furloughed" resonate differently for each person and carry a range of emotions and connotations. These specific words significantly impact our self-perception and how we perceive others' views of us. They affect our ability to move forward both professionally and personally. It's not just about being laid off or fired; it's about how we discuss it, explain the reasons behind it, and navigate through the experience. We all know that words hold significance, and the way these particular terms are employed during such a critical moment carries power and meaning.

In 2021, Ed joined my weekly career coaching group after being laid off from his job. I admired his presence, commitment to his family, and contributions to the group. He really knew how to express vulnerability and authenticity about what it felt like to be furloughed and subsequently laid off. I valued his transparency. Discussing being laid off, fired, or furloughed is challenging. However, what stood out to me the most was the way Ed illustrated how certain words about losing his job profoundly affected him and his family. I appreciated how he healed from this experience and what he learned from it.

INTERVIEW WITH ED: "LIGHT AT THE END OF THE TUNNEL"

I devoted twenty years of my life to this company. It was a law firm with sixty locations and 1,800 employees. As the architect and a facilities manager, I expanded it from twenty offices to forty offices on my own. Then, we began hiring project managers to work alongside me. The team grew from forty to sixty offices. It was my passion. I felt truly good about it, and I was respected. It was very rewarding to witness the firm's growth. I took great pride in what I had achieved.

I called my boss for a scheduled call at 2:00 p.m., and he said, "Okay, we've decided to furlough you. Please put your phone down and turn off your computer. Thank you very much. We'll send you a box tomorrow, and you'll put your computer and all company items in it and return it to the firm." I said, "I have a meeting at 3:00 p.m. Should I do that?" He replied, "No, you should just stop what you're doing right now," and that was that. I quickly contacted my team and said, "I've just been furloughed." I also discovered that several others had been furloughed throughout the company.

When I spoke with my team, we all felt uneasy about the situation. I told them, "Look, they have to keep people. They still need people here when somebody calls and needs something for the facilities department." Ultimately, the company ended up outsourcing everything and eliminating my position. With the pandemic, it was very easy for them to claim it was due to COVID.

They used the word "furlough." It wasn't. The emotions when I found out I was furloughed were different from those I experienced three months later when they laid me off. The **furlough** gave me hope that I would be able to return. However, when I was **laid off**, it was that sense of *wow—it's done*. Laid off meant no more opportunity, no more hope.

There was never a sense of relief when I was laid off. It always felt like failure. What did I do wrong? Did I fail my team? It was more personal and more about **me**. It wasn't until I talked about what happened with others who had gone through similar situations that I realized I needed to look at the big picture. It was planned. It was simply part of the business process.

My wife was working from home the day it happened, and my daughters were also at home due to the pandemic. They heard my call with my boss and recognized from the tone of my voice during the conversation that something was wrong. I hung up the phone, looked at them, and said, "I've been furloughed." And my family cheered. My youngest daughter made me a card and wrote, "Congratulations on your furlough." We prepared a fancy meal and had champagne with dinner. They sang, "Happy furlough to you." They were so relieved that I had been furloughed because COVID was so stressful, and they witnessed how much it affected me. It was such a challenging situation trying to manage sixty office locations during the pandemic. They were so concerned for me and relieved that I didn't have to endure that stress anymore.

I cried when I told my wife I had officially been laid off, and she hugged me. The other shoe had finally dropped. It was final. When I was furloughed, we had discussed whether they would invite me back, and she had asked, "What will you do when they invite you back? Are you going to go?" Of course, I would go back. But it felt different when I was let go. The crying and the hugging were just the finalities of it. But it was also a release of grief.

WERE YOU LAID OFF, FIRED, OR FURLOUGHED?

What comes to mind when you hear the words "laid off," "fired," or "furloughed"? For many, there's a roller coaster of emotions: anger, frustration, fear, financial uncertainty, and countless unanswered questions about what comes next. Ed's story really resonated with me, and with others who needed to understand they are not alone in their feelings. It is important to understand the distinction between being furloughed, laid off, and fired, not only to know what these terms mean for you individually, but also to aid you in moving forward successfully. There is a psychological aspect to this due to a significant amount of shame, guilt, and internal judgment associated with being laid off or fired. I experienced the shame, guilt, and self-judgment—not from others—and I understand the toll it can take on you.

We often hear the terms "laid off," "fired," and—more recently, especially during the pandemic—"furloughed." While these words ultimately mean you are out of work, it's important to use the correct terminology.

According to Money.USNews.com, "Being fired means you are terminated from your job due to something that the company deems was your fault. If you are laid off, that means the company deems that they are at fault . . . Being furloughed means you are still employed by the company you work for, but you cannot work and cannot receive pay. The difference between being furloughed and being laid off is that a laid off employee would have to be rehired to work for the company again. If you are furloughed, you may still receive employee benefits and you may be eligible for unemployment during this time."[3]

As someone who has been laid off, just hearing that being laid off means the company is at fault definitely takes the sting out of it, and I wish more people would talk about it in those terms. I believe that if it were stated at the time of the layoff that the company is at fault laid off employees would feel less ashamed and guilty and would remove internal judgments. Even though I was laid off and not fired, for a while after it happened, I still felt like it was because I was at fault and had done something wrong. I questioned everything about the work I had done, my identity, who I was, what I was capable of, and what people thought of me. Once I could reconcile being laid off with what it really meant, I shifted my thinking and realized I did nothing wrong. Reducing the work force resulted from poor decisions made by the leaders of the organization, and those choices ultimately impacted many people and the organization as a whole.

Thankfully, being laid off doesn't carry the stigma it once did. I believe a large part of this shift is due to the mass layoffs we experienced during the pandemic and how "normalized" it has become. It was easier for people to say, "I was laid off because of COVID," and nobody would ask any questions. However, whether you are laid off or furloughed, it still feels very personal, and that's okay. It's still a hard pill to swallow. You hear those words, "We no longer need your services, or we are reorganizing, or your position has been eliminated," and the sting and shock are still very real. You will still question, "Why me, and not someone else? Why was I chosen?" However, it is important to remember that it is not your fault. Whether you are furloughed or laid off, *it is not your fault*. Remembering that is the first step in the healing process.

THE MYRIAD OF REASONS FOR BEING LAID OFF, FIRED, OR FURLOUGHED

Understanding why you were laid off—and not just in vague terms—is crucial for the healing process, moving forward with your job search, and ultimately for gaining closure. I believe that simply reviewing this list will help you better understand your situation and hopefully provide you with peace of mind and clarity, especially if you are uncertain about the cause. If you work in an "at-will" state, companies aren't required to disclose a reason, and that can leave you without a sense of closure. Hopefully understanding some of the common causes will help you develop a plausible rationale for your layoff so you can begin healing.

Causes of Layoffs:
- Downsizing
- Reorganizing or restructuring
- Mergers or acquisitions
- Change in business
- Loss of funding such as grants, donations, etc.
- Loss in revenue
- Position is eliminated, or role is redundant
- Outsourcing

Meaning of "Furloughed":
- Temporarily relieved from work without pay
- There is an expectation that the worker will return to work
- Benefits will continue during the furlough

Firing Offenses:
- Poor performance
- The job was not a good match for you
- Misconduct
- Abusing time off
- Unethical behavior
- Illegal behavior
- Broke a rule in an employment contract or company policy

Your Rights After a Layoff:
- *Note: These will be different for every company and every state*
- Severance package (if this is not offered, ask for one)
- COBRA health insurance
- Outplacement services to assist in finding a new job
- Unemployment benefits
- Accrued vacation time payout.

Your Rights After Being Fired:
- *Note: These will be different for every company and every state.*

- Your final paycheck (deductions may apply.)
- Potentially eligible for severance
- COBRA health insurance
- Potentially eligible for unemployment depending on circumstances.

Below is a checklist to follow if you have been laid off or fired, ensuring your protection and well-being. This will also vary depending on the company and state, so make sure to do your research. You can contact the Department of Labor for more information. It's crucial to ask questions.

- Know your rights
- Get everything in writing
- Ask about severance
- Ask about your retirement – 401(k) or 403(b)
- Investigate healthcare coverage options
- Determine the details of your final payment
- File for unemployment
- Compensation for unused vacation time
- Agreement on the messaging for the reason you have left the company/organization
- Providing a reference or letter of recommendation
- Copies of your performance reviews
- *REMEMBER, DO NOT SIGN ANYTHING*, such as a termination agreement, until you have read everything thoroughly and had an attorney review your documents, particularly if you are asked to sign an NDA or a non-compete agreement.

REVISITING ED

I received tremendous support from my family and a group of others who had also been laid off. That group helped me to heal. Seek support in any way you can and ask for help because you can't do it alone. Without it, you risk becoming embittered when you're on your own, and it can get ugly. Those feelings can become internalized. It's like thinking you don't want therapy, but then you go and discover how beneficial it can be. If you're hesitant about therapy, find someone to talk to—it doesn't have to be with others who have also been laid off; it can be anyone.

Discussing everything helps remove the emotional weight. I know many people struggle to talk about being laid off, and while I can only speak for myself, I associate it with a sense of failure. So much is tied to our jobs—many of us define ourselves through our work. I am an architect and a facilities manager; that is my identity. Therefore, when that is taken away, what do I say? When I tried to explain being furloughed and then officially laid off, I found it difficult to do so without feeling compelled to clarify that I had been very successful in my role. I achieved a lot while there, but the firm made a business decision to head in a different direction. I received a severance package and moved on. I knew I had to leave it at that. Otherwise, it becomes overly emotional. This is why we need to have these conversations about being laid off. It helps you process the experience and gain the necessary perspective.

As a result of the layoff, I became much nicer and more considerate. I showed up and was present for my family. There were other internal and external changes as well. My relationships with people changed. I now take the time to engage more with others and really show interest in their well-being. Before this happened, everything revolved around the office, impacting my relationships at home. My wife told me it hurt to see me changing because of the job. After getting laid off, I started to pay more attention to her. I finally began to appreciate her more. The depth of my relationships with others improved. I started to structure my conversations differently and they actually had substance. Before, I tried to connect in a meaningful way, but it often felt superficial. My focus was solely on work and the next project I needed to tackle.

In thinking about what comes next, I'd like to be more soulful with the people I interact with. It'll be interesting to see if I can achieve that or if I revert to merely checking the boxes and continuing to move on. I appreciate the idea of finding something more meaningful and creating a civic good. That would provide great satisfaction and fulfillment from participating in those roles. I am seeking passion rather than just collecting a paycheck and going through the motions of my responsibilities. Just knowing there's hope at the end of this, whatever that might look like.

WHERE IS ED NOW?

One of the jobs Ed applied for, which he was passionate about, was to be a diplomat for the United States of America. His daughter was interning at the Department of State and sent him the link to a facility manager position. It required a lot of work, studying, and interviewing, but he is now a facility manager in an exotic country, representing the USA and promoting security, prosperity, inclusion, and women's empowerment. This is Ed's dream job, and he recognizes and appreciates what a long, strange trip it's been!

READER ENGAGEMENT

The purpose of this section is to assist you if you have been laid off or fired, to ask the right questions to ensure your protection, to understand what is happening, and to navigate through the situation that has occurred.

- Do you fully understand why you were furloughed, laid off, or fired? If not, how can you obtain that information?
- How will you prioritize your mental health and self-care now?
- Do you have a support system to help you during this time? If so, who are they?
- What tools and resources are available to help you navigate through this time?
- Have you asked for help? How can you ask for help during this time?
- Are you comfortable discussing being laid off or fired? If not, what would help you have this conversation?
- Do you have all the information from your company regarding the layoff? This includes details about the severance package, available benefits, unemployment information, health insurance (COBRA), and any other potential eligibility.

CHAPTER 3

The Impact of Being Laid Off

Unfortunately, layoffs are becoming increasingly common. Companies tend to default to the belief that conducting more layoffs and reducing staff is the best option when addressing financial problems. But is that truly the best solution? Or is it merely the quickest and easiest way out? Are companies genuinely considering the collateral damage caused by layoffs? Are they mindful of the human capital that will be affected? Are CEOs and leadership truly exploring alternatives to layoffs? Why aren't executives willing to reduce their salaries, forgo their base pay, or furlough staff instead of opting for immediate terminations? What message is being communicated to the staff? Are they demonstrating that employees matter? Is the bottom line the most important factor, or is it the message that executives can continue their lavish lifestyles without interruption?

Not all companies approach layoffs in the same manner. Many manage them with empathy, decency, understanding, and support, offering resources to those affected. This approach clearly helps lessen the impact on individuals who have experienced such a traumatic event. In this chapter, you will meet a client of mine who courageously shared her story about being laid off, how it impacted her in ways she never imagined, and how it affected her kids. We will explore how layoffs are not created equally.

Instead, view this experience as an opportunity to navigate your life in ways you never imagined. Embrace your own story and narrative. Use this experience to learn about yourself, what is important to you, and what you want to do next. Most importantly, I want you to find peace and happiness and offer yourself grace and kindness.

INTERVIEW WITH CLIENT A.: "ONLY YOU KNOW WHAT'S BEST FOR YOU."

My role was Director of Professional Relations, which meant I was responsible for developing strategic partnerships and managing customer relationships. At the time, my manager, the president of our business unit, was retiring in December. Due to a new reporting structure, the new president removed me from the executive leadership team, where I had served for the past three years, and placed me under a VP. I was in the process of revamping programs, strategies, and structures that defined my role and the organization. I received approval from my manager and the immediate past president to continue with my initiatives. This was a challenging period as I navigated internal politicking and collaboration.

I wanted to get everyone on board with what the previous president and I had agreed upon as the new direction for my role's strategy. I had secured agreement from everyone else, but the new president remained hesitant, and we needed his full support. My current manager encouraged me to proceed, saying it was great. So I did. I continued implementing additional steps to

revamp and reinvigorate our entire structure. However, I began receiving conflicting messages from different vice presidents within our organization. The VP of
marketing said I had half the budget I needed, while my
manager and another VP reassured me not to worry and
that we would find the funds. Keep moving forward.

It all came to a head about a week and a half before I was laid off. For the first time, my manager paid
attention to what I had been telling him about how dire
it was if we didn't secure the funding. I met with the VP
of marketing and my manager and said, "You guys, if I
don't get more money, we don't have advisory boards
and partnerships with external societies. We don't have
all these things I've been working on." Both of them replied, "Okay, let's put a plan together." I compiled everything and inquired about presenting it to the president.
They said, "I don't know if we've got enough time." However, all the budget numbers had been finalized. After
that conversation, I had a light bulb moment. I realized
something was off. That's when I went online, cashed in
all my company incentive points, and prepared myself
for a potential layoff. That was on a Monday. The following Tuesday, I had been texting with my manager, who
was lamenting about not being able to take a day off,
among other things. He was trying to take the day off
but had been called into the office for meetings. Around
5:30 p.m. that day, I received an email from my boss with
a meeting notice that included someone from employee
relations. I knew exactly what was coming.

I immediately called him, knowing he probably
wouldn't answer, and he didn't. But I still felt like I had
to call him. After that, I completely broke down with my
husband and skipped the bedtime routine with the kids.
I was a mess. I was group texting with my girlfriends.
I got out a lot of the "Oh, shit," shock kind of stuff—
and shock is a perfect word for it. I was physically con-
vulsing and shaking. I was freezing. I was like, "What is
happening to me?" I've never had that sort of physical

reaction to something before.

The next morning, I called in for our scheduled meeting with my manager and employee relations. Having been on the other side of these conversations, I tried to remain stoic and professional. Still, it's much more humorous when you know they're reading from a script and that they must cover all the talking points. The conversation lasted fifteen minutes. As I listened to what they were saying, especially what my manager was saying, it struck me just how impersonal everything felt. Just the day before, we had been texting and joking about plans for the following week, and now he was reading from a script. I realized I would never talk to him again. He never called me afterward, nor did he send an email. There was nothing. That was it. That was at 11:00 a.m., and I had until 10:00 p.m. to get everything off my computer before losing access to it all.

I had to buy a new phone and computer, which I did on the first day, and then I shipped all my stuff back to corporate. I was very thankful to be working remotely. During a layoff, working from home is a silver lining. I didn't have to make that walk of shame out of the office; I just turned everything off and dropped it off at UPS.

There are mixed reviews from people about layoffs, especially when they occur remotely. My experience involved a one-on-one conversation, thank goodness, unlike those horror stories where 5,000 people are on a Zoom call, and they say, "If you're on this call, you're no longer needed." Having had tough conversations with individuals, I understand the importance of keeping personal feelings aside. It must be strictly business. And it can't be a personalized conversation—even though that's what you crave, as you become just another number, a casualty of business.

I received a large packet of information about my separation agreement. Additionally, I got two months of continuous service and received my two-month salary. I postponed looking through all the information, including details about COBRA, because I knew I had two months to review it. I needed to be in a better frame of mind to examine it without feeling bad about myself. Many different emotions and realizations come from this experience. Now, I carry a new label because I have a different identity; I am officially "unemployed."

I was in a bit of shock during that call. I have gone through restructurings before. The company had undergone a complete enterprise restructuring three or four years previously, and I was one of the few people who led the entire effort for our business unit. So I had experienced this before and understood where the decisions were coming from. What I felt most during that call, though I couldn't name it at the time, was a sense of betrayal. I had invested so much into this business and faced numerous challenges from a professional perspective.

After I was let go, I felt very strange. I immediately called my husband and texted all my friends, "Yep, I was right. They let me go." I called my team to inform them. I had to admit to them that I didn't know what would happen to them, but I wanted them to hear from me that I had been let go.

I was fine when I called and told people I had been laid off. I kept my composure, except for one person. I had a meeting scheduled with some of our customers and one of our external partners about two hours after I was laid off, which I had to cancel. I sent him a text message saying, "Hey, I can't make our call. I'm going to need to cancel." I left it at that. He immediately contacted me and said, "We're working to get customers on the phone. We spent three weeks setting up this call. Why are you canceling at the last minute?" Instead of texting back, I accidentally called. Thankfully, I knew him well. We've worked together for the past fifteen or twenty years. I was a wreck, just bawling on the phone with him.

That night, I went home and told my children. My daughters were seven and ten at the time. My husband

and I discussed how we would tell them. We just sat them down and told them. Having that conversation with them actually helped me the most. Their reactions were, "You're gonna be home more? We get to hang out with you more. We get to spend more time with you. You won't be traveling. Can you be a chaperone for my field trip?" They saw it all as a positive, whereas I viewed the layoff negatively.

My older daughter is very reflective and perceptive. She asked, "Are we going to be able to stay in this house? We just bought a cottage, Mom. Will we still be able to have that? You have a new car on order. Will we still be able to have the car? What about all these things?"

My husband stayed home with me the day after I was laid off. I needed to keep busy, so we went out, indulged in some retail therapy, and then he returned to work the following day. On Friday, I kept myself occupied by exercising and watching some movies. My oldest ended up staying home from school that Monday and Tuesday. She was largely trying to make sense of things. It felt like her life was being uprooted or disrupted as well. For her, just spending time with me was what she wanted and needed. I knew she wasn't really sick. We ran errands, watched movies, and hung out for two days. It was great.

MY TRANSITION AND TRANSFORMATION

In the first few days and even the first couple of weeks after being laid off, I allowed myself to sit and do nothing when needed. Soon after being laid off, I contacted a career coach. I knew I needed something like a stake in the ground because I wanted to move on, and I recognized I couldn't sit and wallow in this self-pity phase forever. I also knew I needed some time just to be. Now, I get up and take a few minutes in the morning to sit and have coffee, eat breakfast after the kids are off to school, watch the morning news, and then work out. I look through the work I am doing with my coach and read various self-help books and books addressing major life transitions. Doing different things to keep myself mentally and intellectually stimulated has given me a bit of hope and optimism for what lies ahead. I am doing a much better job of volunteering at the kids' schools and attending all their events and activities. It's been nice to have the time and flexibility. My days are different now, and I am trying to understand how I once had time for a full-time job given how full my days are now.

There are good days, bad days, and everything in between. Now I'm going to get emotional. I want to be a tremendous role model for my girls. It's been great for me to realize that and to have my oldest verbalize it. It scares me how much she's like me. She found a quote the other day where someone was talking about how people will tell you you're crazy to leave a really good job to follow your passion. She showed it to me and asked if it looked familiar. She's recognizing that I'm trying to figure out what I want to do while balancing what's good for the family with what I really need at the same time. I was talking to her about a job that interested me. I swear, she is ten going on twenty-five. She said, "That sounds really interesting. You get to do what you want, and it's still something similar to what you were doing. But it sounds more fun, and you get to do good." It makes me feel like I'm doing something right with her if I can have this conversation with my ten-year-old, and she understands the value of doing something for the greater good.

I feel like I'm moving in the right direction. It reinforces the thoughts and feelings I've been having, both personally and professionally. I'm figuring out where this path will lead me. I still don't know what will come next, and the idea of stepping into a new role that I don't know anything about is quite intimidating. However, I can aim for something greater than where I was or explore something new, as I now have a clearer understanding of my strengths and weaknesses. I'm excited about what I'm discovering about myself.

NOT ALL LAYOFFS ARE CREATED EQUALLY

You read in chapter 2 about the differences between being furloughed, laid off, and fired. Depending on the category you fall into, this can impact how you move forward and navigate the process emotionally, physically, financially, and professionally. When we say that not all layoffs are created equally, we mean that various conditions can arise and multiple factors influence the decision to initiate a layoff. Not all layoffs are created equally regarding their reasons or how they are conducted within companies. We initially began hearing about mass layoffs in the tech industry, before they spread to other sectors.

- According to a Challenger, Gray, and Christmas report, companies planned a total of 721,677 job cuts in 2023, marking a significant increase of 98% compared to the previous year, making it the highest annual total since 2020.[4]

- Companies cut 761,358 jobs in 2024, according to a new report from career services firm Challenger, Gray & Christmas, with the technology, healthcare, and automotive sectors leading the way, though cuts were far more widespread across industries in 2024 compared with 2023.[5]

- "Companies underwent extraordinary change in 2024 due to rapid technological advancement and shifting economic conditions. Most employers are anticipating additional uncertainty with the upcoming administration, which is leading to slower hiring and more layoffs in the short term from various sectors."[6]

The numbers are overwhelming. So how do we recover from this? Companies will likely not be the same. More importantly, how people view work, invest, and engage in their jobs have changed forever. It can take up to two years to heal from the psychological trauma of losing a job. As a result of COVID, the landscape of remote and hybrid work has changed significantly. How people communicate and conduct their work has shifted, and we had to quickly figure out how to make this arrangement functional and maintain this structure.

Unfortunately, layoffs occurred during COVID and the only option out of necessity was a virtual layoff, but that doesn't lessen the impact on those affected. If anything, it has created fear and anxiety among employees. That feeling when you receive a meeting notice, typically scheduled for around fifteen minutes, is now something we all recognize. It often leads to a brief meeting, usually a five-minute conversation, and then, within fifteen minutes, access to email, Slack, and communication channels is abruptly cut off, ending your job. If this has happened to you—and unfortunately, many of you reading this know exactly what I mean—you might have experienced an inability to communicate with colleagues. You don't get to say goodbye or process what has occurred; for many, there is no closure regarding the situation.

My layoff as you know, was conducted with the CEO and HR in an office with glass walls where everyone could see, and it was shocking and devastating. But at least I had time to pack up my belongings, send a few emails, and say my goodbyes. It wasn't easy, but I was one of the lucky ones compared to others. You can't help but wonder why and how someone is chosen. Why were others spared but not me? Catherine Tran wrote an article for LinkedIn in 2023 that captures the experiences many endure during such events. Her article mentions that business journalist Natasha D'Souza has been laid off twice. D'Souza observes that "taking it personally holds you back from creating mental space and emotional energy to reorient yourself to a new identity and navigate this new exploratory phase in your career," she then continues, "instead of stewing in the emotions that come with making it personal, it's more productive to channel that emotional force toward unlocking avenues for future growth."[7]

I am glad Catherine shared her experience of being laid off. "Getting laid off is an unfortunate event in life that just happens, and at times, very unexpectedly. It's important to keep your mental health in check; take a breath and take it one day at a time. There will be days filled with stress and sadness, but that is the best time to reach out to your support system and loved ones and try to understand that this is just a setback. The universe is ushering you to close the door so you can make room for better things that lie ahead of you." We are not alone in this; we don't have to go through this alone, and there isn't a right or wrong way to feel about it. You will be okay, you will get through this, and you will come out on the other side.

THE EXPANDED IMPACT

Many who have been laid off feel that the layoff is their fault, carrying the blame with them. There is also a belief that those spared from being laid off are more valued. We think we were laid off because of something we might have done, but this is simply *not* true.

I conducted a total of thirty-one interviews with people from diverse backgrounds—male and female, young and old, and everything in between—across various industries and stages of their careers. I discovered consistent patterns and insights that surprised me, while others made perfect sense and were entirely expected. However, what I found particularly interesting was the difference in responses among millennials, GenX, and Boomers when dealing with layoffs. Their emotions, perspectives, and mindsets varied significantly, more than I had anticipated.

I found that Baby Boomers, GenXers, and older Millennials had a stronger emotional connection and reaction to being laid off. It felt more personal and targeted, and the recovery process took longer. It was far more overwhelming and shocking, especially for those who had worked for their companies for a long time and had developed their careers there. Their identities were much more intertwined with their jobs and careers. Many described their jobs as their entire identity; it was all they knew. The thought of losing that sent them into an identity crisis. The idea of reimagining who they are, what would come next, and how to move forward was daunting and paralyzing.

The younger Millennials have a different perspective and approach regarding their expectations of work and finding the next job. They were able to transition to a new job much more quickly. In their view, a layoff is just a part of working, and staying at a job for only a couple of years is normal for them.

Therefore, their emotional connection and engagement in their jobs differ significantly.

Understanding the impact of being laid off is crucial. The effects of layoffs are significant and far-reaching. In fact, it's challenging to find a better word that truly captures the power of the experience of being laid off. I recently encountered a compelling definition of "impact," and I believe it perfectly relates to our discussion. "The resulting effect, positive or negative, that the actions we take have to change the physical or mental state of others around us—and therefore have the power to change the future path of an individual or group."[8]

We've discussed the how, why, and where of layoffs, and now we will explore the impact so you can understand and process how it feels, how to respond, and ultimately, how you can move forward. The effects of layoffs can be felt in many areas and have far-reaching consequences for employees, the company, and the broader economy. A layoff is a jarring experience both at the moment it occurs and in the months that follow.

POTENTIAL IMPACT FOR LAID OFF EMPLOYEE

- Financial
  - › Loss of pay and/or benefits
  - › Challenges finding a new job
  - › Dipping into savings or emergency funds, taking out loans, or increasing credit card debt
- Physical
  - › Stress-related symptoms
- Psychological
  - › Feelings of isolation, disconnection, rejection,

shame, guilt, failure, embarrassment, loss, grief, and lack of closure
> Questioning your value, self-worth, and ability to contribute to another company
> Questioning what others will think, why you were laid off, how you will tell people, if you'll be okay
> Blaming yourself for being laid off, thinking you should have done something different.

POTENTIAL IMPACT ON THOSE WHO SURVIVED THE LAYOFF

Companies should not overlook the employees who stay after a layoff. Many of you may have experienced this and understand how things can shift dramatically following a layoff.

- Increased expectation to pick up the slack of those who have left
- Lack of messaging and transparency about what happened and the real reason(s)
- A lack of messaging about why people should stay includes clear roles for you, benefits, and expressing appreciation for the value that people bring
- Lack of support or empathy from leadership, manager, etc.
- Business as usual attitude, without time to process what has happened

IMPACT ON COMPANIES

- Reputation of the company:
  - › Lack of trust and transparency among employees, stakeholders, and consumers
- Impact on company morale:
  - › Feelings of uncertainty and anxiety among remaining employees
  - › Loss of productivity
  - › Survivors' guilt
  - › Heightened stress on layoff managers
  - › Obtaining or managing talent becomes a challenge
- Financial:
  - › Drops in shares
  - › Reduced consumer spending
  - › Unexpected financial impact: severance and health benefits add up

In one way or another, we are all part of a layoff. As long as layoffs remain an option for companies, they will continue to happen and will always be a part of how companies function. However, the more knowledge we have about why, how, where, and when events like this occur, the better we can equip ourselves, care for the survivors, and support the companies. This improved understanding will help us mitigate the negative impact and provide more support, understanding, and resources for those affected.

REVISITING CLIENT A.

I am learning that I was more of a mentor and a leader than I initially thought. Hearing from members of my team after they learned I was laid off—comments like, 'Oh my goodness, I've appreciated what you have done for me throughout my time working for you,' or 'You have taught me so many things. Thank you'—was incredibly impactful. In hindsight, I recognize that I am learning what others have already seen in me, even when I couldn't see it in myself. I always felt recognized or rewarded by upper management because I received promotions and more responsibilities. Still, I never considered the perspectives of my employees or peers. So that's been a positive revelation. This experience has made me aware of my impact on the company, my team, and the external influence I didn't realize before my layoff.

My advice to someone going through a layoff is don't act until you are ready. I needed more time to prepare for the next steps. I found this quote from organizational psychologist, Adam Grant, whom I admire. It was about major life decisions: 'On major life decisions, the purpose of seeking advice is not to get answers. It's to gain perspective. No one knows what's best for you. They can only share what makes sense to them. The most important question to ask is not what you should do. It's what you might be missing.' That quote sums it up for me. No one knows what's best for you. Do the work to figure out what's important for you and what's best for you before you're ready to act.

WHERE IS CLIENT A. NOW?

Client A.'s story truly highlights the effects a layoff can have on families, especially children. They perceive and experience this impact through a different lens, and their processing of certain situations and information differs from that of adults. They offer a unique perspective and evoke a profound emotional response. We get up, go to work, and support our families every day. But do we take the time to consider how major life transitions affect our children and their ability to understand what is happening?

In the first few months following her layoff, Client A. was firmly against working in the same industry. She wanted to explore anything and everything as long as it was outside her previous area of expertise. As time passed, she realized that she genuinely enjoyed the type of work she had been doing, and it was more about the constraints imposed on her that often led to her frustration and discontent. Once she felt prepared to re-enter the workforce and began responding to calls and offers for assistance from her network, she became more energized and excited about job opportunities in the industry again, but on her own terms. Ultimately, she founded her own consulting firm in the industry she had been in before her layoff, which allowed her the flexibility to also focus more on her family.

READER ENGAGEMENT

This section aims to help you navigate your layoff experience and reconcile your feelings about it. Hopefully, you'll feel equipped with tools and resources should you ever need them. You can also share this information with others you know who are experiencing a layoff.

- How are you taking care of yourself?
- What have you discovered about yourself since being laid off?

- What advice would you offer to someone who has been laid off?
- Is there anything you wish you had done differently after your layoff?
- How can you prepare and protect yourself if you experience another layoff? What could you do differently? (Hopefully, you won't need this!)
- How can you advocate for yourself and your coworkers before, during, and after a layoff?

CHAPTER 4

The Three-State Recovery Process

There is so much happening in the world right now. When I began writing this book, there wasn't a pandemic, a mass economic downturn, the highest unemployment rates and mass layoffs, global protests against systemic bias and racism, the insurrection on January 6, or a political landscape that has turned this nation upside down. Much more can be added to this list, and it is just as significant.

All of these things affect everyone in various and profound ways—mentally, emotionally, physically, and financially. We have all been impacted by at least one of these aspects in some way. We are enduring a lot, and it would feel different if we faced just one issue at a time, but so much is being thrown at us all at once with no end in sight. We are being tested in ways we never imagined. We are asking many questions with few answers, limited guidance, and sometimes very little hope.

Given everything that is happening and what will continue, how do we take care of ourselves? How do we create space and make time to engage with our thoughts and emotions, and how do we forge a version that resonates with us now? Are you allowing yourself to be present, to slow down and quiet the noise around you? Are you tapping into your inner wisdom, trusting yourself, and showing up for those around you? When we do this, we foster stillness, which in turn brings the clarity we all need and the actions necessary to feel better, avoid feeling stuck, and move forward.

We often overlook the importance of rest, recovery, and resetting after a layoff. When faced with challenges such as injury, surgery, or loss, we prioritize our rest and recovery because our bodies need it to heal and move forward. Do you truly reflect on the rest and recovery that your mind and body require when facing mental or emotional struggles?

After reading this chapter, I hope you gain a new perspective on the importance of rest and recovery, as well as their benefits for both your mind and body—not only for yourself but also for those around you. Doing so will help you reaffirm your identity, regain your confidence, and carve out a path to rediscover who you are and who you aspire to be as you move forward.

*****

I met Dianne in my weekly coaching group. She is nearing the end of her career, has gone through several layoffs, and has first-hand experience of what a layoff feels like during critical points in her journey. She clearly understands how it has affected her and her family, and she emphasizes the importance of taking care of oneself mentally, physically, and emotionally. She highlights the significance of rest, recovery, and resetting, which we will explore in this chapter. Let's examine Dianne's interview to help you start thinking about your own rest, recovery, and reset.

INTERVIEW WITH DIANNE: "LIFE HAPPENS, WHAT DO WE DO WITH IT?"

On Thursday, September 12, 2019, my career underwent a significant disruption. By that, I mean I was informed that, due to changes at my then-firm, I would be forced into a situation known as RIF, which stands for reduction in force. I was not surprised, considering the series of events from the previous year leading up to this moment. Still, it was a little unnerving for me because, at this stage of my life, I was hoping to continue my career for another four or five years, making this a sudden upheaval. However, it was also a relief due to the overwhelming feelings I dealt with each day going to work and facing my superior. It felt like a huge cinder block had been lifted off me. Although witnessing such events is common, it is still surprising because it resembles a death. You know it's coming, but when it happens, it's like, "Oh, boy. It is the end. The finality." Yet, when you consider the other side of things, you think, "Okay. It's not so bad. I'm going to be okay. This is how it has to be. I'm okay."

I felt fortunate because someone from the IT department came to my office to give me a heads-up. So leading up to the actual dismissal, it wasn't shocking. Once I learned I was being let go, I immediately began packing up my office, and that's when I received the initial call. It wasn't earth-shattering. I was very prepared. During the call, they said, "As you know, the firm has been going through some changes, and I'm sorry, but the firm is going in another direction, and unfortunately, it does not include you. We will be terminating your services due to a RIF." I replied, "I understand."

After the layoff occurred, I immediately called

my husband. When I told him the news, he was quiet. That evening, I asked him how he felt when I shared the news, and he replied, "Empty." I asked, "Why?" He said, "Because of you, I felt empty." He continued, "I felt shocked, disbelief, and empty." I replied, "You knew I *hated the bastard*, so I'm glad I don't have to report to him anymore." After that, he said, "Well, you know what? If you're good, I'm good." I assured him, "I'm telling you, I'm good." I also explained that I felt relieved. My reaction eased his mind because he understood my trepidation about going to work every day and what I had to face. So that night, it wasn't sadness, it wasn't bewilderment, it wasn't anxiety; it was pure relief. I felt as if I had won the lottery or Mega Millions. I wouldn't describe it as "overjoyed" or "excited." It was simply relief. I felt an overwhelming sense of relief.

The next day, I realized that for the first time in eleven years, I was without a job, and a bit of a reality check set in. But then I reassured myself, "I'll be okay." I felt happy because I no longer had to stress about the unknown at this stage in my life. I would be alright, come what may. I told myself that I needed a little time to unwind mentally and physically to deal with what lay ahead of me.

When you experience a disruption in your career path, as I did, especially later in life approaching retirement, it's crucial to pause, take a moment, breathe, breathe, breathe. Focus on what you want to achieve at this stage of your life. If you're considering throwing in the towel, determine the course of action leading to that decision. If you plan to return to the workforce, as I did for medical benefits, establish a timeframe to jumpstart this process.

Several months after being laid off, I began to unwind. I rested. My body felt much better, and my mind was in a good place. Because I took the time to rest and recover, I am now more patient and accepting of the unexpected changes that can occur at any moment. I have the ability to assess and handle these situations more calmly rather than succumbing to worry, which had previously led to anxiety and anxiety attacks. I learned to manage my anxiety by reminding myself, "It's not the end of the world. It's okay. I'm going to be fine." My thoughts are calmer, and I feel significantly less anxious.

REST AND RECOVERY ARE ESSENTIAL

Recovery is a crucial aspect of this process, especially regarding job loss. We recognize the importance of healing from illness, surgery, addiction, or any traumatic experience in our lives, as well as from the effects of a long, intense workout. Our bodies and minds need rest to recuperate effectively. This necessity applies to everyone, but especially those who have been laid off. We are living in uncertain times, which can be emotionally and physically draining.

If we allow ourselves to rest and recover, we become more creative and productive, make better decisions, and enhance our problem-solving skills. We present the best version of ourselves, feel more energized, and gain increased clarity. We all share the same twenty-four hours; the question is, how are you utilizing this time? How are you caring for yourself and those around you? How do we recover after experiencing a loss like this? Everything you've known—your identity, your daily routine—has just been taken away and disrupted. Recovery will look different for everyone. It is not a one-size-fits-all situation.

What is Rest and Recovery?

Let's begin by defining the terms "rest" and "recovery." While it may seem obvious, I want us to explore how each is connected to the experience of being laid off and why this is important. When an event like this occurs, we often feel an immediate shock, as well as anger and devastation, which is completely normal. Now, reflect on how your body, mind, and emotions reacted when you were laid off and what you needed to recover.

Recovery is a word that some consider taboo because we often associate it with addiction or illness. But why must it carry a negative connotation? Can't we view it positively? I googled the word recovery, and I found the various definitions intriguing. Merriam-Webster's Dictionary defines the first as "a return to a normal state of health, mind, or strength." The second definition is "the action or process of regaining something stolen or lost," and the final definition is "the process of combating a disorder (such as alcoholism) or a real or perceived problem."[9] These provide interesting perspectives on what recovery means. I appreciate the first two definitions as they relate to being laid off—the dust settling, returning to a normal state of mind and strength, and reclaiming something lost. All of this resonated with me as I reflected on my layoff, how my mind and body reacted, and how I navigated this experience.

How do *you* manage feelings of being overwhelmed, cultivate resilience, prioritize your well-being, and find meaning when a traumatic, life-altering event occurs? Below are steps to focus on rest, recovery, and resetting. When you feel comfortable and ready, remember to move on to the next steps. This process is not linear for everyone.

STEP 1: PAUSE – DON'T PANIC

The initial and automatic reaction is to panic when an event like a layoff occurs. Believe me, I understand this all too well. A flood of emotions, thoughts, and feelings washed over me, and I had a brief moment of panic, thinking, "Oh shit, I don't have a job. How am I going to pay my mortgage?" I knew deep down that I would be okay and that I would not be alone in this.

After the layoff, take a moment to evaluate what you have and what you need. This helps put things into perspective and allows you to feel grounded, centered, and able to breathe. Once the dust settles, process the situation. Step back and assess everything, giving yourself time to understand what has happened. Most importantly, remember that the layoff was not your fault; it is the company's responsibility and should not define your self-esteem or value; it is not a reflection of your work or who you are as a person.

STEP 2: REFLECT – ASSESS THE SITUATION

Keep in mind that assessing the situation isn't linear; there's no fixed timeline, and it depends on which version works best for you. Breaking this down into micro steps will make it feel less overwhelming and more manageable.

- 2a. Allow yourself the time and space to reflect. Establish a regular schedule for self-reflection to uncover your true desires and determine your next steps. Don't confine your reflections to your job; consider your entire self instead.
- 2b. Recuperate: Allow your mind and body the time and space necessary to rest and rejuvenate.
- 2c. Acknowledge what is in your control and what is beyond it.

- 2d. Focus on your breathing. Losing a job can greatly impact your life.
- 2e. Take care of yourself. You are not on a schedule for rest and recovery. There doesn't need to be a timeline; just let this unfold naturally. Focus on your sleep, nutrition, exercise, and connections with others.
- 2f. Embrace your fear, frustration, and worry by talking to friends, family, or others, and avoid isolating yourself from them.
- 2g. Acknowledge your feelings, but don't allow yourself to become stuck in them.
- 2h. Feelings of shame, guilt, and embarrassment are just that—feelings; they are not facts.
- 2i. Identify what you truly need, instead of depending on what others assume you need. Only you have the power to define this.

STEP 3: MOVING FORWARD

Every client I work with, including myself, has gone through and will continue to undergo this recovery process. When recovering from a job loss, we focus on the emotions, physical aspects, psychological effects, routines we are accustomed to, financial components, and ultimately, establishing new routines and daily practices that support our next steps. Recovery involves exploring who you are and who you aspire to become.

MY PERSONAL EXPERIENCE WITH REST AND RECOVERY

My recovery from losing my job occurred in various phases. When it first happened, there was tremendous devastation, but then the realization of what had occurred set in, bringing me relief. It felt as though the heaviest weight had been lifted from my shoulders, freeing me from the need to pretend; I didn't have to live as the person I had created due to my misery and how I presented myself at work every day. I also experienced a physical recovery. I never realized how much tension I carried in my shoulders, pulling them up toward my ears; I was constantly clenching or contracting some part of my body (you know what I'm talking about and how this feels). I was always incredibly tense; even while sitting on the couch watching TV, my hands were balled into fists. After being laid off, my shoulders relaxed, I stood taller, wanting to be seen, and my body was no longer constantly clenched. It's amazing how much better we feel without realizing the stress we carry in our bodies and how profoundly it affects us when we are in a constant state of stress and unhappiness.

When I worked at my old job, I developed significant stomach issues and was constantly sick. Doctors couldn't determine what was wrong with me for the longest time. I underwent endless tests for years and received no answers. Finally, I found an amazing doctor who figured it out. I remember him telling me one day, "It is not realistic to eliminate your stress, but you must find a better way to cope with it." The night before I was laid off, I was sick all night; after I got laid off, I didn't see my doctor for an entire year. During that time, I wasn't sick, and my body finally recovered.

I also remember feeling physically exhausted all the time. Once I left that job, I wasn't constantly tired; I regained my energy and became active in my life again. I was finally showing up as the person I aspired to be. I allowed myself to rest, recover, and reset. I listened to my body, heart, and mind for the first time. For a long time, I neglected this. I know it was my choice not to do so, but once I paused, took a breath, opened my eyes, looked around, and reassured myself that I would be okay—and actually believed it—I began to change, open up, and see myself in a new light. I also let others in and allowed them to see me as I wished to be seen.

NOT JUST FOR AFTER A LAYOFF

We've been discussing the importance of rest and recovery during a layoff, but I don't want to overlook how crucial it is while you're currently working, when life gets stressful, or when you feel burned out not just because of work. Rest and recovery are vital, no matter what's happening in your life; our bodies and minds need it. What do doctors advise when we have a cold, the flu, or whatever it may be? We require rest and recovery. Ultimately, this is about taking care of ourselves, presenting the best version of ourselves, and recognizing when it's time to pause, acknowledging our need for a break, recharging, and reinvigorating ourselves to carry on with life.

As essential as rest and recovery are after experiencing something traumatic or significant, we don't have to wait until we reach that point. Rest and recovery can occur at any time and should be integrated into our lifestyle. I also want to emphasize that you don't need to wait until you reach a breaking point and feel completely burned out. As you explore the importance of rest, recovery, resetting, and reinvigorating yourself, let's look at those options. Do you know what resources are available at work to manage your stress and burnout?

TAKING A SABBATICAL

If you could take four months or six weeks off work, and it was paid, would you do it? Do you know what a sabbatical is? Have you ever considered taking a sabbatical from work? Did you know it was possible? These are important questions that need to be explored and answered. Elizabeth Perry, a writer for betterup.com, shared in her 2023 article, "According to one survey, paid and unpaid sabbatical benefits have become more popular between 2016 and 2021 . . . In fact, most organizations thrive more when employees take breaks. Sabbaticals benefit both the individual and the employer. They offer growth opportunities and the chance to learn new skills, which can make you a better employee."[10]

Here is another case for taking a sabbatical and why more employees and companies are considering it. I came across an article on worldatwork.org, written by Nu Yang, who shared that "Conversations about work sabbaticals have even reached mainstream media. In January 2022, the *Wall Street Journal* published an article titled 'The Sabbatical, a Power Move for the Burnout Era,' documenting exhausted employees who, instead of joining The Great Resignation, decided to go on a sabbatical."[11]

WorldatWork researched and found that "interest in sabbaticals is growing among employers . . . The report found that out of a total of 886 responses, representing U.S. organizations of various sizes and across multiple industries, 10% said they offered paid sabbaticals to their employees (in 2016, it was 8%). Out of 580 responses, 29% of organizations offered unpaid sabbaticals (in 2016, it was 18%)."[12]

With rising rates of burnout and employee turnover, companies are realizing that offering sabbaticals may be a more effective strategy for retaining talent and reducing disruptions. Instead of the much-discussed "Great Resignation," employees are now opting for sabbaticals as an alternative. This approach is less drastic and supports company culture and morale by allowing individuals to step away from their jobs and return rather than resigning.

We often equate sabbaticals with those in academia, but that perception has changed over time. More people are considering taking a sabbatical, provided their company allows it. So, what is a sabbatical? It is a long break from work, separate from vacation or regular leave, usually granted after an employee has spent a certain number of years with a company. People can take sabbaticals for various reasons; it ultimately depends on how you define it for yourself.

Who is eligible to take a sabbatical? Typically, this is granted after five or more years of employment. Generally, this consideration is reserved for more senior staff and is sometimes viewed as a reward. As we learn more about sabbaticals and they become more commonplace, various reasons for taking them emerge. There are benefits for both the employee and the company if this option is available. It's important to note that a vacation, sabbatical, and mental health break are different and should be treated separately. Here is a list of some of the most common reasons people take a sabbatical.

- Job Satisfaction: When you've been in the same role or with the same company for an extended period, you might feel that your work lacks meaning, or you may experience mental fatigue. Don't get me wrong; people also take sabbaticals when they are happy with their jobs.
- A break: Taking time away from work can be a transformative experience.
- Volunteer Opportunities: If you're passionate about a cause, consider volunteering your time to make a meaningful contribution.
- New Project: This can be referred to as a working holiday, during which someone works on a specific project, possibly a passion project.
- Personal and professional growth: an opportunity to acquire a new skill or work toward a personal milestone and gain clarity about what you want next in your career.
- If you are thinking about taking a sabbatical, here's how to plan and request it:
- Check if there is a sabbatical policy at work. If there isn't, make your case for one; they might consider it. Determine whether it is paid or unpaid so you can plan accordingly.
- This is not a decision to take lightly. Conduct your research first to understand what a sabbatical

entails. The more information you gather, the better prepared you will be for the conversation.

- Identify your reasons for taking a sabbatical and evaluate whether this is financially feasible for you.
- Assess the impact of taking a sabbatical on your job.
- After finalizing all the details for you and your family, submit a formal request.
- Determine the best time to take it.
- Organize all necessary arrangements and outline the details of this time off.
- Make sure all projects, deliverables, and assignments are organized while you are away.

OTHER OPTIONS

It is not guaranteed that your company will approve a sabbatical, even if it has a sabbatical policy. If this happens, don't make any drastic moves, such as quitting your job; instead, explore other available options. If your need for a break centers on resetting and taking care of your mental health, consider taking a mental health break instead, or possibly a disability leave. If you are trying to negotiate this, flexibility is essential. Work with HR and your supervisor to determine what makes the most sense for you.

I have recently been working with more clients who are on disability or mental health leave due to feelings of stress, anxiety, depression, burnout, and underperformance. They feel their work is suffering, and their mental health is being severely impacted. They recognize that they need to reprioritize and find ways to achieve better work-life integration, as work-life balance isn't realistic. Taking leave like this requires the involvement of a doctor or mental health professional. These are just a few options for taking leave or time off. If this type of leave is not accessible to you, consider taking an extended vacation. If that isn't feasible, is there flexibility in your work schedule? It is always important to inquire about what you are entitled to and what options are available, and most importantly, *always advocate for your needs*.

As you can see, rest and recovery are essential and come in different forms, varying for each individual. I can't emphasize enough the importance of taking time after a traumatic experience to reconnect with your emotional, mental, and physical needs. The day after a knee replacement, you wouldn't go for a run; instead, you allow your body the time to heal, regain strength, and adjust to what is necessary for proper recovery. If you are willing to care for yourself physically, why aren't you willing to do the same for yourself emotionally and mentally? Although the physical and emotional effects differ after a layoff, your life has been affected, and you want to contemplate your next steps to move forward with clarity when you're emotionally and physically ready, making the adjustments you need.

REVISITING DIANNE

You might be wondering what happened to Dianne, who has been an advocate and a shining example of mental health awareness since I first met her. After her most recent experience with being laid off, here is what she had to say:

MY ADVICE TO OTHERS

You're going to be fine. Stop thinking it's the end of the world just because you've been laid off. It may sound cliché, but it's true — things happen for a reason. It's not about the money; it's about how you feel about what you're doing and whether you're happy doing it. Yes, I earned a very good salary, but that salary came at a cost of stress and anxiety. Which would I prefer? The latter. I would rather have peace and be comfortable. I would prefer to be in an environment where I'm happy to go to work.

A layoff affects other people, not just the individual it is happening to. As long as your family sees and knows you're okay, it brings them relief because they observe you're not depressed, and you're not introducing anxiety into the living space or the relationship. They need to recognize your capabilities, mental state, and resilience. One of the things my daughter said to me was such a lovely compliment: "Mom, I know you'll be okay. You always find a way, which is one of the things that makes you so great."

MY RESET

There is a stigma associated with discussing being laid off. Some people feel guilty and worthless, as if it's their fault. Shame is attached to it. What did I do? You didn't do anything wrong. I didn't do anything wrong. You need to acknowledge what happened and discuss it. Hey, it happened to me, too. I turned it around. Look at where I am now. It can happen to you, and if you do these things, you can steer your own course, and you'll be fine. However, you won't be fine if you sit, dwell, and do nothing. Maintain a positive perspective. It's about your entire mental outlook. Sometimes, you have to go through a situation like this to realize how resilient you are, to see that you possess strength, and to understand that everything will be fine. Never lose sight of your self-esteem and your motivation as a person. More importantly, don't let an unexpected disruption in your life defeat you. Learn and grow from it.

WHERE IS DIANNE NOW?

Due to the disruption caused by COVID and the dismal job market at that time, Dianne quickly explored other avenues to stay engaged and generate income. Today, she is a successful licensed real estate agent working for a religious institution. She no longer faces the challenges and demands of corporate work, nor does she harbor resentment or disdain for her job or supervisor. She understands that sometimes in life, one must turn a setback into a comeback. Always be prepared for the inevitable; this way, the fall will not be fatal. Life is good!

READER ENGAGEMENT

This section aims to help you envision alternatives for addressing the stress, burnout, and feelings of disconnection from work that you may be experiencing. These questions should encourage you to think creatively and explore ways to create new opportunities for yourself.

- How do you take care of yourself when feeling overwhelmed, stressed, or anxious?
- How can you ensure you are resting and recovering when necessary?
- Are you aware of the physical and emotional signs that indicate your mind and body need rest and recovery? How do you prioritize these needs?
- Do you see your layoff and this time as an opportunity or a hardship?
- Are you working to recover from your layoff, or are you just learning how to move forward?
- If you have the ability to take a sabbatical, or to

take a break before finding a new job, what type of
sabbatical would you like to take?

- What is the best way you can structure a sabbatical
to maximize its benefits?

CHAPTER 5

Can You Recognize Burnout in Yourself?

Burnout affects both the workplace and the individuals within it. This concept was first introduced in the 1970s but it still poses a challenge even during stable periods, let alone during stressful ones. However, we are now experiencing it in unprecedented ways, leading to collateral damage. Nearly every aspect of our lives is affected by stressors that have heightened everyone's risk of burnout. At some point in our lives and careers, we have all felt its impact. We recognize that burnout and stress are pervasive, and unfortunately, they show no signs of disappearing anytime soon, even becoming the new norm. The positive news is that burnout is preventable. You (and your employer!) can take steps to prevent it through adequate support and an understanding of its causes. We can create workplaces that promote employee well-being, and managers and organizations can implement measures to avert workplace burnout. Given that you have recently experienced, or are currently experiencing a layoff, this is the perfect time to consider these issues and create a plan to incorporate them into your life going forward.

Given the current landscape of toxic work environments,

poor leadership, mass layoffs, and dissatisfied employees, companies are scrambling to retain their workforce and ensure that their employees feel happy and engaged. Organizations need to better understand and address the stress and burnout their employees face. Companies cannot sit idly by, hoping that circumstances will resolve themselves and improve. Statistics reveal the troubling reality of burnout, stress, and employees leaving their jobs. I am astonished by the number of clients I have worked with lately who are quitting their jobs without securing new positions, driven by overwhelming stress and feelings of burnout. Moreover, several clients have taken mental health leave or disability leave for these reasons. They are using this time to reevaluate their work, their lives, and their aspirations.

How did we arrive at this point?

This chapter will focus on identifying burnout in yourself and others, as well as supporting both you and those who are experiencing it. By the end of this chapter, you will have practical steps to address your burnout, and if you are managing a team or individuals, you will be prepared to assist them.

The interview for this chapter is essential for anyone who has experienced burnout, stress, anxiety, or depression as a result of work. Natalie's story is compelling because she demonstrated bravery in advocating for her mental health and in asking herself tough, honest questions about her well-being and what she needed to take care of herself. It was crucial for her to be truthful and acknowledge that she was not okay and needed help. Her interview will guide you through her journey, illustrating how burnout affected her mentally and physically, how her relationships were impacted, and, primarily, how it changed her. She will also share how she navigated the process to obtain the help she needed and how to advocate for herself.

INTERVIEW WITH NATALIE: "ADVOCATE FOR YOURSELF."

I would describe it as a snowball effect. I was working nonstop, and the workload continued to increase with no end in sight. I had just launched three international campaigns simultaneously as part of one workstream across three markets. A week before the launch, I traveled to Tokyo to shoot a fourth campaign and was forced to execute it in parallel, without any project management support. The scale of launching three campaigns while shooting a fourth and managing four different time zones was unreal. I felt like a hamster on a wheel. I didn't sleep; I just kept running.

Typically, there is some downtime between projects, though not much. Unfortunately, unexpected creative issues following the launch required round-the-clock, cross-team resolution, which was intense and highly stressful. I was running on fumes, leading the effort while navigating the challenges of a new manager and team dynamics. Once resolved, my new manager presented me with an unrealistic work plan, making me feel like I was set up to fail. What was even more concerning was my awareness of how difficult it would be to manage. In the face of the impossible, my instinct was to "paddle like hell to keep the boat afloat!" Ultimately, my effort to meet the overwhelming expectations pushed me into overdrive and burnout.

In high-pressure situations, I get tunnel vision, unable to see the forest for the trees. I focus on executing and delivering results. I have always been able to bet on myself; I've been described as "a rock in a rough ocean," someone who delivers under the toughest circumstances. However, this felt like running a never-ending marathon. I barely ate and worked 24/7 just to keep going. The stress consumed me. I didn't realize how little I was eating; I was so frantic and focused that I often forgot to eat. My anxiety made sleep nearly impossible. In short, I was a frantic mess. Usually, I'm highly active; I enjoy being with my partner and seeing friends and family, but I retreated and became a shell of my former self. I felt depressed and highly irritable. I could never wind down or relax; I was constantly exhausted. None of it was healthy, and I knew I had to make some changes.

Advocating for yourself is important; while you may not receive the support or justice you desire, knowing that you fought back matters. I documented the events leading to the current circumstances and reported my manager to HR. I provided background information and my current workload, along with solid evidence regarding the scale, scope, and timelines to illustrate the ongoing situation and to pursue a reasonable resolution. I was aware that HR was not on my side, but I knew I had to take proactive steps to demonstrate that I had documentation, understood my rights, and would not tolerate any disrespect. Recognizing that I was taking action brought me solace. It also helped me reframe my perspective and realize that there's only so much I can control and perform effectively. This is not my failure; it is simply a result of being treated unfairly.

Looking back, I should have approached HR sooner to discuss the events that had transpired and the ongoing hostile work environment that followed over the past year. I could have gotten ahead of it, played the game, and taken control of the narrative earlier. Instead, I tried to be a good team player and addressed the issues directly with my manager, who ultimately couldn't be trusted to do the right thing, and I ended up paying the price.

MY DECISION TO TAKE LEAVE

Human Resources took a month to conduct an internal investigation. While their findings concluded that the events did not constitute what they labeled a workplace violation, they acknowledged it had been a challenging year. They gently reminded me of my options for leave and provided additional information. I expressed the need for a clear, reasonable, and achievable plan. After taking a day to decompress, I returned to meet with my boss to review the work plan. I thought, let's reset and see if we can return to normalcy.

In hindsight, that was a significant mistake. I should have realized that my manager was determined to see me fail. He orchestrated and exaggerated the charges because he was implicated in the recent campaign issue and intended to make me the scapegoat. The unreasonable workload was a tool to carry out his plan to push me out.

Most importantly, I should have prioritized my well-being. I was stressed and burnt out, yet desperate to keep my job. For two more months, I pushed forward, but my situation only worsened. I was meeting the plan's requirements, but my manager consistently offered subjective criticism, told me my work was "below the bar," and contradicted me. I tried to obtain clear objectives and KPIs (key performance indicators), but the work wasn't solely about delivering on time or receiving positive feedback from colleagues (which I did). Much of it was open to his interpretation, which was the whole point (and his intention). Ultimately, he held all the power.

During those two months, I hadn't been sleeping or eating, and I had lost even more weight. My relationship suffered, and things began to crumble. I found myself asking, "How can I continue like this?" "What do I risk by trying to keep going under these overwhelming conditions?" Reflecting on these questions, I realized I had to take a leave immediately.

At first, I worried, "What will people think?" I thought, "I can't let my team down or burden them with my work." However, I realized that I'd been there for almost two years, and during that time, I had consistently delivered and managed complex tasks. People knew I was not someone who failed to meet expectations. Ultimately, the company will always care for itself. Everyone is replaceable, and the work will still get done. You shouldn't be concerned about what others might think or say; their opinions are irrelevant. They know nothing about your situation.

You also can't make good decisions when you're in a crisis. You must decompress, be present and mindful, and work through the situation. Ensure you have a plan for your return to work, be honest with yourself about your needs, and prioritize putting yourself first. While on leave, planning how and when to return to the office is critical. From a mental health perspective, I met with my doctor and therapist to align on how many days a week I would be in the office and how many hours per week I would work. She wrote a letter to my employer outlining these terms, which my company later accepted. Knowing my employee rights had been breached, I contacted a lawyer to assess my case and discuss the next steps regarding legal action. Leaving provided me with the space to refuel and prepare for the upcoming fight. It also allowed me to regain my composure and confidence. I was not going back without protection; having a strategy and being clear about the next steps made me feel empowered and safe.

*****

Now that you've read the first part of Natalie's story, I hope it has inspired you to reflect on your own well-being and mental health, the experiences you've had at work or are currently facing, and the importance of seeking help, knowing that you are not alone. Next, let's delve into the depths and impact of burnout and explore ways to address it. This is your opportunity to examine your current surroundings and situation, assess your levels of stress and burnout, and develop a plan that will support your progress in a healthy and productive manner. Are you ready to be honest and confront the tough questions?

Let's start with what employee burnout is. "In 2019, the World Health Organization (WHO) defined employee burnout as an occupational phenomenon that occurs because of unmanaged, chronic workplace stress. The WHO also laid out the three criteria required for work-related stress to be classified as burnout. The employee must experience: 1) Flagging energy and/or exhaustion, 2) Increasingly negative feelings toward their job and/or increasingly feeling distanced from job responsibilities and workplace operations, and 3) A downturn in professional efficacy."[13]

A Gallup report attributed the five main causes of burnout to:
- Unfair treatment in the workplace
- Workloads that are unmanageable and/or unrealistic
- Lack of clarity regarding job expectations
- Poor communication and support from the management team
- Unreasonable deadline.[14]

Here are some hard facts that illustrate the current landscape of burnout and stress in the workplace. "The American Family Life Assurance Company of Columbus (Aflac) conducted a study between August and September 2022, finding that most

US workers experience burnout. Thirty-six percent rated their level of burnout as moderate, 15% as high, and 8% as very high." These levels of work-related burnout are significantly higher than those reported in 2021 (nine percentage points more) and two percentage points higher than 2020 levels."[15]

Unfortunately, we have all experienced this far too often. Is this just the norm, and what companies are building into their culture? What do you want to do about this, and how do you want to manage your job and career moving forward? Are any of these impacting you, the people you manage, or anyone you know?

- Work-life balance is in jeopardy.
- The most "financially fragile" are the most burnt out.
- Burned-out employees are struggling with mental health issues.
- Job satisfaction, performance, and employee retention are negatively affected by burnout.
- Employee well-being programs aren't being utilized.
- Shift-based industries have some of the highest rates of burnout.
- One of the main causes of burnout? Your boss!

We all recognize how much time we need to allocate to different people, our jobs, and various aspects of our lives. However, for many of us, this can sometimes get out of balance. Our perceptions of what we should do, must do, and want to do often differ from reality. We must ensure that our expectations, perceptions, and results align, because when they do not, we can experience burnout. The bottom line is that burnout can affect anyone in any career; it does not discriminate, and all jobs hold the potential for stress and burnout.

RECOGNIZING BURNOUT

Burnout isn't a medical diagnosis. Some experts think that other conditions, such as depression, are behind burnout. Researchers point out that individual factors, such as personality traits and family life, influence who experiences burnout. Whatever the cause, job burnout can affect your physical and mental health. Consider how to identify if you're experiencing job burnout and what you can do about it. The below questions from the Mayo Clinic are valuable questions to ask yourself to determine if you are showing symptoms of job burnout:

- Have you become cynical or critical at work?
- Do you drag yourself to work and have trouble getting started?
- Have you become irritable or impatient with co-workers, customers, or clients?
- Do you lack the energy to be consistently productive?
- Do you find it hard to concentrate?
- Do you lack satisfaction from your achievements?
- Do you feel disillusioned about your job?
- Are you using food, drugs, or alcohol to feel better or to simply not feel?
- Have your sleep habits changed?
- Are you troubled by unexplained headaches, stomach or bowel problems, or other physical complaints?[16]

The signs of burnout are obvious in some people but subtle in others. It's important to help others recognize when they show signs of burnout. We must care for ourselves and one another. Sometimes, we cannot see it in ourselves, so others may not notice when they are burned out, either. Here are some signs that indicate people might be struggling to manage their stress and are moving toward significant burnout.

- Low energy
- Declining productivity or job performance
- Often looking worn out or run down
- Increasingly negative attitude about your job, boss, or company
- Frequently mentioning feeling stuck, stressed, or overwhelmed

SUPPORTING YOURSELF AND OTHERS

Rebounding from burnout and preventing its recurrence requires three things: replenishing lost resources, avoiding further resource depletion, and finding or creating resource-rich conditions going forward. Monique Valcour wrote a great article in Harvard Business Review about steps we can take when we begin to feel burned out. She wrote, "To get back to thriving, it's essential to understand that burnout is fundamentally a state of resource depletion. In the same way that you can't continue to drive a car that's out of fuel just because you'd like to get home, you can't overcome burnout simply by deciding to "pull yourself together."

Up to this point in the chapter, we have focused on recognizing what burnout looks like and whether you are suffering from it. Now, let's discuss what you can do about it. You always have options, and you don't have to face this alone. If you had a cold, the flu, or another medical issue, you would take care of yourself and, if necessary, consult a doctor. Caring for yourself when you are burned out, stressed, anxious, or overwhelmed is just as vital and should be a priority. If anything, we have learned that ignoring these signs and symptoms can lead to more significant problems and serious consequences. We must manage our priorities to avoid the physical and emotional exhaustion that leads to burnout. If you are already experiencing burnout, these steps can also aid in your recovery. The recommendations below aim to help you prevent, cope with, or recover from burnout.

- **Don't ignore the signs of burnout:** You might think it will just go away on its own, but that's not how it works. The consequences of burnout can be serious and may have mental, physical, or financial effects.

- **Assess your current situation:** You might already know what contributes to your burnout, but sometimes it's necessary to identify the root of the problem. Reflect on your work and home circumstances and pinpoint the indicators of stress. Where do you feel the most stress, and what is the source of that stress? Consider what drains your energy and what replenishes it. Once you recognize the factors leading to your stress, burnout, and exhaustion, you can determine the steps to take moving forward.

- **Consider all your options:** Talk about your choices at work with your boss to find out what is available to you. After that, discuss your options at home with your family or anyone else you believe can assist you.

- **Ask others for help:** You *don't* need to tackle this alone. Inform your boss, co-workers, family, friends, or a medical or mental health professional about what is going on. Be specific about your needs when seeking assistance. You can't assume that people are aware of your situation unless you speak up.

- **Self-care:** Make self-care a priority. I understand you are busy, but it's essential for your well-being, including your mental and physical health. It's not just about finding time but about creating time for yourself.

- **Make sure to exercise and stay active for your body:** This doesn't have to be a grand gesture; it can be as simple as walking for a few minutes to get the blood flowing. Other relaxing activities, like yoga or meditation, can also help. Whatever helps you manage your stress and take your mind off work should be included.

- **Establish a healthy sleep routine:** Obtaining adequate sleep is vital, particularly during this period, as it aids in restoring well-being. We all acknowledge the significance of sleep.

- **Recovery Time:** You can be intentional about your rest and recovery. After a major project or significant deadlines, or if the workload is overwhelming, take time to recover. Allow yourself a break before diving back into everything. Discuss this with your boss and ask for their support.

- **Don't spend all your time at work:** Set boundaries. Allow yourself to take breaks throughout the day, seek help if necessary, and keep open communication with your co-workers and boss about your needs and feelings.

- **Involve yourself in other areas of your life:** Consider reframing your mindset about your well-being. Assess your work situation, pinpoint the sources of stress and burnout, and make any needed adjustments. Reflect on your well-being, what it entails, and how you can achieve it. Remind yourself of your purpose at work and your reasons for being there. If home and family issues contribute to the problem, try to reevaluate your circumstances there and, once again, make any necessary adjustments.

- **Stay connected with others:** This is a great time to talk to people about what you're going through and how you feel. You will find that others share similar experiences. Social contact is also crucial, allowing you to focus on things in a variety of venues other than work. Engage with others socially to help reduce stress. Look for activities that will help lower your stress. Make time for yourself; don't wait for it to happen on its own.

- **Set Boundaries:** Establish clear distinctions

between work and personal life. Leave your work behind. Create both mental and physical boundaries. Don't hesitate to use the word "No" when setting limits. Feel free to decline invitations when necessary. If you're feeling overwhelmed at work, discuss the option to say "No" with your boss while offering alternatives.

REVISITING NATALIE

At the beginning of the chapter, you read the first part of Natalie's story about how she became burned out and how it affected her mentally, physically, and emotionally. Here is the rest of her journey. Hopefully, after hearing her story, you will take the time to stop, reflect, and ask yourself honest questions about your own burnout and its impact on you.

ON CREATING A CULTURE THAT SUPPORTS MENTAL HEALTH

The topic of mental health has long been considered taboo, but remember, you are not alone. Disability benefits exist for a reason—it's not solely for physical conditions. People will respect your courage to advocate for yourself by prioritizing your well-being and mental health. Consider what matters most: your values, health, well-being, and your ability to perform at the level required by your job. If you don't feel comfortable saying, "I am taking leave for mental health reasons," that's perfectly fine. It's entirely up to you what you choose to share regarding your reason for taking this leave. People were very supportive when I returned, but honestly, they wouldn't have cared if I didn't return, either. No one knows what you're experiencing. Ultimately, the only opinion that counts is yours.

ON MOVING FORWARD

Now I am establishing better boundaries both personally and professionally. I will be more self-aware and in tune with my needs and mental health. Having regained a healthy work-life balance, I will evaluate companies closely to ensure they offer a work-life balance and have a culture that aligns with my values. I am also reassessing the size of an organization and the type of role I wish to pursue. My last experience taught me a lot about what I do not want and that I should take a different approach when evaluating the role, the team, and the company as a whole.

I will continue to advocate for myself and seek help when necessary. Prioritizing my mental health and well-being is essential. Staying in touch with my doctor, my therapist, and my coach will remain a priority to maintain balance and focus on the people, activities, hobbies, and work that bring me joy. I will not overwhelm myself with a job again. This experience has served as a harsh reminder that you are the only person who can take care of yourself. You alone are responsible for your happiness. My greatest responsibility is to myself, not to my work.

WHERE IS NATALIE NOW?

At the time of the interview, Natalie's journey was still relatively fresh. She is in transition, working on her career plan and strategy while taking time to determine her next step. She has taken on some consulting projects, and she is networking with trusted colleagues and friends to explore companies of interest. She is mindful of enjoying this corporate break because she knows it's much needed. Natalie stated, "Sometimes in life, you need a break, and stepping off the corporate ladder is more than okay."

READER ENGAGEMENT

It has become increasingly clear that burnout and stress are significant aspects of our personal and professional lives. We are doing our best to cope with these challenges and recognize that we cannot—and should not—navigate this journey alone. Seeking help is a positive step that should be integral to our healing process. Throughout the chapter, you read about the signs and symptoms of job burnout, as well as practical strategies for addressing it. Many questions were raised throughout the chapter, so let's focus on the next steps to help you move forward.

- Can you recognize when you're burned out? Do you know what signs to look for?
- Do you plan to deal with your stress when you feel burned out?
- What does your plan look like?
- Do you know the signs of burnout and stress with your team and co-workers?
- Do you feel equipped to support someone who is experiencing burnout and stress?
- How can you talk to your boss when you feel burned out and stressed?
- What gives you energy, and what depletes your energy?

CHAPTER 6

Your Transition and Transformation Journey

L ife happens. So what are you going to do about it?

Now and then, we are faced with a significant force of change. These events reshape our lives, often in ways we cannot even imagine and with an intensity we cannot control. When confronted with a challenge, such as a sudden disruption in our lives—be it divorce, job loss, death, miscarriage, or whatever—we quickly discover who we truly are, what our values entail, what is important to us, what we are capable of, and how resilient we can be. Unfortunately, it often takes disruptive events like being laid off for us to re-evaluate our lives. During times like these, we must reflect on what truly matters and discern what is necessary and what is not. We center our lives around our job, intertwining our personal and professional identities, but when we lose a job, everything can change in an instant. So what happens when everything shifts in a flash, and what can these changes teach us? We understand that we enter these changes one way and emerge on the other side as a different person.

Life is unpredictable, and while most of us tend to plan ahead, we can't always do so which can create a lot of stress. It reflects our desire to be and stay in control, and when this is inter-rupted—or should we say, disrupted—by a job loss, everything gets turned upside down. The fear of the unknown generates sig-nificant stress and anxiety, especially after being laid off, as we face uncertainty about what will come next or how long it may take to find the next job. People often struggle with uncertainty, allowing their minds to drift to worst-case scenarios and create negative possibilities instead of focusing on the positive.

We should become comfortable with the uncomfortable. This is one of the best ways to continue advancing yourself. Learn to accept the uncertainty in your life; the more you do so, the less stress and anxiety you will experience. Uncertainty is simply a part of life. Embrace the unpredictability and focus on the present; you are exactly where you need to be.

This chapter will focus on how change shapes our lives and how to transition after a layoff or other unexpected transforma-tions. In this interview, the storyteller wished to remain anony-mous, but he still wanted to share his experiences because he felt many of you could relate, and he did not want you to feel alone.

INTERVIEW WITH CLIENT B.:
"WHERE IS THE CHOICE IN ALL THIS?"

I worked as a flight attendant for a luxury airline. It was a start-up airline with only forty-eight business class seats flying from Europe to London, and I was proud to be promoted to the training department to lead flight attendant boot camps. While living in Montreal, I had to relocate to New York. On the day I was laid off, I was scheduled to conduct a training flight and needed to leave at 7:00 a.m., so I had to arrive at the airport ear-ly. The night before, around 11:00 p.m., my phone started blowing up.

My phone just kept ringing and ringing and ringing, and finally, somebody sent a text that said, "What's happening?" At 11:30 p.m., I finally spoke to someone who told me, "We're out of business," and I replied, "That can't be right. I'm running this flight tomorrow. There's no way." I opened my computer and went to the website, and it said, "We've ceased operations." I just kept thinking, "What the hell?" It was so unexpected. Then, in the middle of the night, I found out I was no longer employed. The official word from the company came the next day, and I didn't even hear it directly from them.

When this was all happening, disbelief was the first thing that went through my mind. It took me about four or five days to process everything. I showed up to work on Monday and stayed on for almost a week unpaid, helping out because I felt that void and needed to do something. I was also experiencing a deep sense of fear. I had been going through many personal changes, and I faced some significant personal setbacks that were quite severe and stressful. I had just been diagnosed with a condition that made me question my self-worth, resulting in a great deal of mental health distress. While dealing with these challenges, I reminded myself, "Well, at least you're working at your dream job, so you have that to look forward to," and that's what helped me get through the move to New York and everything else. This really clarified how much my self-esteem and identity were intertwined with my work at this company.

Several things happened during that time, and the biggest was that I was frantically searching for a job. I was only unemployed for three weeks before I jumped into a role at a hotel. It was an easy hire, and I took it out of fear. It was March or April of 2008, and this hotel job was meant to be a temporary solution to give me some time to figure out what I really wanted to do. A couple of months later, the recession hit and the job market deteriorated. I spent three miserable years working at this hotel because there were no alternatives.

After being laid off, I knew people who said, "Well, the first thing I'm going to do is take some time off. I'm going to go home and think about things. And I'm going to really take my time before I take the next step and think about things logically." I kept thinking, "That's kind of reckless. How can you do that? What about security, and how will you pay the bills?" I had just moved to New York, where the rent was three times as much as I paid in Montreal. I kept thinking, "How can you take time? Time is a luxury you don't have right now. I need to get working." In retrospect, that time is something I needed but didn't take. The lesson learned: if I ever find myself in the same situation—which I hope I don't—I should take the time and figure things out. If I had taken the time, I might have done things differently, but I can't say for sure. I was twenty-nine at the time, and self-awareness at that age isn't necessarily at its peak.

The job market worsened during the three years I was at that job. I kept thinking there was no end in sight, and I needed to start shaking things up. I knew I needed to do some soul-searching, but I also knew I wanted to stay in the training field, which I really enjoyed. Everything in the airline industry was a mess, so I knew I wouldn't work in that sector again. I applied for hundreds of jobs in training-related positions, and the competition was just ridiculous. I realized I needed to upscale myself and put myself in a different league. The first thing I did was volunteer work, which was training-related. I could list this on my resume, and I was giving back to the community.

I also considered returning to school to bridge the gap. Returning to school felt intimidating as an adult, so I signed up for a Certificate in Training Management. A side story about being laid off from the airlines influenced my next steps. When the airline shut down, we received our last month's paycheck more than a year later. There was also a settlement involved. There's something about the WARN Act: when they conduct mass layoffs, they are supposed to provide a ninety-day warning, but they didn't do that for us. As a result, we received a settlement that paid for school. I took the first class and loved it. I completed the certification in a year, but I wanted to keep learning, so I went to grad school for Industrial Organizational Psychology. I found my passion.

My coach training institution is very important to me, and I'm proud of it. However, it's not the entirety of who I am, which is something significant to acknowledge. Here are some of the lessons I've learned throughout this experience: you can't tie yourself to just one thing. I've learned to differentiate between my identity and my biography. I recognize that while individual performance may fluctuate over time, self-worth remains constant. Performance varies, and things happen, but there's a core part of me that will stay the same and support me through challenges. I'm not confident in everything I do, and I question many of my actions, and I will always continue to ask questions. That's the best way we can learn.

If my 2019 self could talk to my 2008 self, there are two messages that I would want to convey. One is, "You're okay just the way you are." And two, "Take it easy. Take a pause. Figure yourself out first before you figure out your external circumstances."

CHANGE SHAPES OUR LIVES

Going through a transition and transition journey can be a tremendous gift. Who knows where it will take you, but it is definitely worth the ride. Change is scary, and people handle it in different ways. I know I am not always good with change, but as I've gotten older, I have learned to appreciate it and try to view it through a different lens. Not all change is bad.

When these changes occur, whether positive or negative, we must ensure we are caring for ourselves both emotionally and physically. This includes managing our mental health, understanding and addressing our stress and anxiety, eating well, and getting enough sleep. Most importantly, we should ask for help when we need it. Even if we don't feel the need, it's beneficial to have someone to talk to.

A change such as being laid off is not a common disruptor. This is a significant life change. Such changes in one's life can lead to upheaval, transitions, and transformations. We like to believe we control the trajectory of our lives, but in reality, we know that isn't true, and life will unfold as it may. There will always be other factors influencing how life progresses. When a major change occurs, we typically take the time to re-evaluate our lives and hopefully confront the difficult questions. We aim to thoroughly examine what is right in front of us. Throughout this book, you've read about the importance of rest, recovery, and resetting—the gift of introspection and how it can transform your life. Now, we will focus on the transition and transformation one experiences during and after a significant life change.

In Bruce Feiler's 2020 book, *Life Is in the Transitions: Mastering Change at Any Age*, Feiler states, "A transition is a vital period of adjustment, creativity, and rebirth that helps one find meaning after a major life disruption . . . ," and he later continues, "Life is never the linear path we might expect or want it to be. We are always going to have disruptions. What has changed is that the number of disruptions is increasing." [17] Felier also asks: "Why do we insist on talking about these periods as something dire and defeating, as miserable slogs we have to grit, grind, or grovel our way through. As long as life is going to be full of plot twists, why not spend more time learning to master them?"[18]

I have spent years working with clients who have been laid off for various reasons. I learned that it's about embarking on the journey of transition and transformation with presence, vulnerability, and humility. Take the time to love yourself, show self-compassion for where you are in the moment, and how you present yourself each day. You need to trust yourself, your abilities, your heart, and your mind.

TRANSITIONING AFTER LAYOFFS

Here is what we know about transitions:

1. Every transition has a beginning, middle, and end, followed by a new beginning
2. They often take longer than you expect
3. The time frame varies for everyone
4. Transitions will occur multiple times throughout our lives
5. Transitions are vital to our lives

Let's begin with the definition of transition. According to Robin S. Rosenberg, Ph.D., in an article from Psychology Today, "Transitions, then, are a time for us to think about who we want to become as part of our lives change. Being in transition offers us an opportunity to reflect on our values (and the ways they may have changed), our goals, and our identities in the different areas of our lives."[19]

Allaya Cooks-Campbell defines individual transformation as "An internal shift that brings us in alignment with our highest potential. It is at the heart of every major aspect of our lives. It affects how we see and relate to the world and how we understand our place in it . . . It can happen in an instant, through a lifetime of development—or, more commonly, through both. The path includes a wide range of transformative experiences that support the whole person. It means prioritizing and consciously developing physical well-being, mental fitness, emotional health, and cognitive agility."[20]

After a layoff, it is natural to ask yourself a series of questions, "How did I end up in this situation, and what do I do now?" Then there are the thoughts about how you transition your life after you've been laid off from what was a normal routine. Your comfort level and your absolutes all change instantly. Even the notion of what it looks like to wake in the morning after you've been laid off and have nowhere to go. Your everyday life significantly changes. This might seem dramatic, but this reality sets in for someone no longer getting up and going to work because their job has ended.

Transitions and changes can happen throughout our lives. While there are negative changes and transitions, we should also remember the many positive ones. These can begin with graduating high school, going to college, finishing college, getting your first job, living independently for the first time, or acquiring your first home or apartment. Other major changes also exist, like getting married and starting a family. All of these are incredibly significant, life-altering, and impactful. Additionally, some transitions and changes can be life-changing in a different sense, having more traumatic and dramatic effects, such as dealing with an illness, going through a divorce, experiencing death, facing a miscarriage, or losing a job. All these changes, whether good or bad, positive or negative, planned or unexpected, can clarify what is truly important in life and foster greater self-awareness, personal growth, introspection, and self-discovery. After a layoff, there is much to consider, from daily routines to broader financial aspects, taking care of your family, and finding your next job. Therefore, the important question is where to begin this process, since you can't tackle everything at once.

Looking back on when I was laid off, I remember that this will look different for everyone; my transition was not what I expected. I learned a lot about myself and surprised myself in many ways. I am someone who likes to plan. I prefer to be in control and want to know what is going to come next. However, during a transition after my life had been completely disrupted and was out of my hands, I had to quickly adjust and be open to change, embracing the discomfort. Most of all, I had to accept that I didn't have all the answers. After all, a life transition is a change or adjustment that will significantly impact your life. I've experienced other transitions in my life, and I have managed to get through each one, but this was different for me. In my previous transitions, I mostly had control, was able to plan, and knew myself going into them. When I was laid off, everything I thought I knew about myself was called into question and, for a brief time, hijacked how I navigated through it. I was in unknown territory. I knew I didn't want to dwell on the emotions that overtook me. I wanted to move quickly through them while doing the necessary work.

I know that for me, the first part of my transition was finally listening to and taking care of my body. I realized I had not been taking care of myself for the longest time, and this really impacted me emotionally, mentally, and, of course, physically. Pausing, resting, slowing down, and acknowledging what was happening around me set me on a good path to being open to what came next. I had become so accustomed to a routine focused solely on work that my entire identity was wrapped around my job, causing me to forget who I was as a person; I wasn't focusing on the whole me. When that becomes your entire focus and then it suddenly disappears, it can be a shock to the system; at least it was for me.

Now that we have started exploring what a transition and transformation look like, let's examine how to embark on this journey. All of these are essential for your transition and your transformation:

1. Take the time to stop and pause, look around, and reflect.

   a. Whether this is the first time you've been laid off or the third, don't downplay how it feels and the emotional toll it can take on you. Even if you prepared for the layoff or knew it was possibly happening, it is still shocking and will take time to process.

   b. It's really important to take care of yourself during this period. Listen to what your heart, mind, and body are telling you. Self-care is essential right now.

   c. Taking this time will help you create a space for clarity and openness to explore whatever will come next.

2. Understand the stories you tell yourself and where they come from.

   a. Are you stuck in the past with your old narrative about who you were, and is the identity you built for yourself affecting how you see things? We all have thoughts that influence how we perceive ourselves and the world around us. This is a great time to start creating a new narrative that focuses on the present and future.

   b. It is up to you to create the narrative, but also recognize that as you change your narrative, your emotions need to catch up with it.

3. Re-evaluate your values and priorities.

   a. Now that you have created the space to reflect and re-evaluate your life. Think about what is important to you, what you need and want, your core values, and how they align with what comes next for you.

   b. Stay in the moment, consider the now and what can come next. You want to avoid getting stuck in your past or you will have difficulty moving forward.

4. Be as intentional as possible.

   a. After a layoff, you will start thinking, talking, and acting differently because you see your life from a new perspective. You will become more deliberate in your planning and the steps you take to move forward.

5. Be present in your life.

    a. After a significant event, it's common to start planning and thinking about what comes next. However, we can often get ten steps ahead of ourselves and miss what is right in front of us, what needs attention. Being present helps you navigate the process toward the next step, but remember, you are exactly where you need to be.

    b. Don't rush it, because you don't want to miss anything. If you are on a journey of transition and transformation, taking the time to reflect, re-evaluate, and reset is important. Embrace all the experiences that come with the transition and transformation.

    c. Appreciate this time in your life and be grateful for it. Consider all the possibilities it may bring, both personally and professionally.

6. Be grateful.

    a. We have so much to be thankful for. It can be hard to see that in the moment after being laid off, and most of us tend to take things for granted, focusing instead on what we have lost. Practicing gratitude can help you cope, reduce stress, and appreciate what you have, opening you up to receiving even more.

7. Ask for help.

    a. You *do not* have to go through this alone, nor should you. Job searching can be daunting, and this transition and transformation journey can leave you feeling very vulnerable. Talking to others who have experienced job loss or similar situations can be incredibly helpful.

b. Identify your community of support. Seeking advice from outside experts can also be beneficial. Relying on those with specialized resources and different perspectives can provide valuable insights.

c. It may also be important to speak with a mental health professional if you find yourself stuck, struggling to process your emotions, or feeling depressed or anxious. These resources can be great tools for your growth and progress.

TRANSFORMATIONS YOU MIGHT NOT HAVE EXPECTED

We know that life changes can be challenging and scary for many reasons, and they can also be exciting at the same time. We hold preconceived notions about what our transitions and transformations can and should look like. However, they don't always unfold that way; some are planned, while others are unexpected. You must manage your expectations, be present, mindful, intentional, and, most importantly, open to the process. You never know where it will take you or where you will end up. To ensure you are holding space during this journey, we have addressed what you can expect, but let's also identify what you might not expect about yourself, the process, and the journey. Hopefully, you have enough information to feel confident in embarking on the process and discovering where it takes you.

- Transitions of any kind can disrupt your plans, sense of purpose, and potentially your role in those plans.
- During this time, you don't have to feel like you must always be happy and productive, or that if you're not actively engaged in something, you are wasting your time. That break or pause is perfectly acceptable. Don't act or respond just because you think it's expected of you.
- You won't have all the answers. That's what this time is for: discovering those answers.
- Transitions and transformations are not easy.
- The reality is that a transition or transformation can suck.
- Transitions and transformations are a part of life. They are not all negative, and it is perfectly fine to celebrate the wins.
- You must be honest with yourself and with others to achieve a successful outcome.
- Vulnerability is just part of it. It doesn't mean you are weak or can't handle what is happening. In fact, it just shows how brave you are.
- There are many new emotions that may arise during this experience. Some you might not have experienced before. Be aware of them, sit in them, feel them, but do not get stuck in them.
- During this time, it is very easy to compare your

life to others. *Stop doing this!* It doesn't serve or help you in any way. Your life is not the same as someone else's.

- Perfect and perfection *do not exist*. Please remove these words from your vocabulary.

NAVIGATING YOUR TRANSITION AND TRANSFORMATION

Navigating through a transition and transformation will look different for everyone. There is no right or wrong way; the timeline differs for each individual, and what works for one person might not work for another. You do you; figure out what works best for you. Remember, it may be bumpy along the way; you might take two steps forward and then two steps back, but you are on a path, and you will land somewhere, somehow. Most importantly, trust yourself throughout the journey.

We understand that there will be both external and internal changes along the way. Change will occur, some planned and some unexpected, but life will go on. Whatever changes are happening in your life, how you choose to respond will set you on your journey of transition and transformation.

In Bruce Feiler's book, he captures and explains life transitions so eloquently that they can be applied to all aspects of our lives: "Life transitions are a skill. Specifically, they're a skill we can, and must, master. Research into everything from habits to happiness has found that if you break familiar processes down into their components, you can engage with these components to achieve a better outcome. Understanding these elements is a precursor to performing it better."

Feiler lays out the seven groupings of tools he has identified for navigating life transitions. As I've said, and Feiler supports this in his book as well, there is no single path through a transition. It is personal to you. The tools he outlines can be used however and whenever you see fit. While Feiler posits that no one uses all seven of these tools, I tend to disagree . . . sort of. No one uses all seven in a single situation, but I think many people will use all seven to some degree at some point in their lives. Different situations sometimes require different tools. If something isn't working, try a different approach.

The seven tools are:

1. Accept It: Identify your emotions
2. Mark It: Ritualize the change
3. Shed It: Give up old mindsets
4. Create It: Try new things
5. Share It: Seek wisdom from others
6. Launch It: Unveil your new self
7. Tell It: Compose a fresh story

REVISITING CLIENT B.

Fast forward a few years—through an acquisition, I found myself back in a corporate job at a large consulting firm. This was the dream job I had always wanted, yet I never thought I would get it. I was so proud of this accomplishment and the big salary that I began to overlook some warning signs. Gradually, I realized that the values in practice at this organization were in direct contrast to my own. I felt stuck and wasn't sure what to do. The economy was in turmoil again, and I noticed a distinct culture of fear. Rumors of large-scale layoffs became realities. This fear kept my peers from "rocking the boat too much" to preserve a lucrative paycheck.

I remembered how my past experience of fear caused me to take the easy way out and make compromises I otherwise would not be willing to make. But reflecting on my past experiences, I realized that this was a compromise I wasn't willing to accept for myself. I did not want to be beholden to fear; I wanted my life's work to be driven by intention and purpose. I took the time to understand that I am okay the way I am, and the disconnect between the organization's values and my own was important for me to recognize. I paused and figured out what was truly important to me. I decided to give up a high-paying job and focus on new ventures that didn't promise a big paycheck, but I had the resiliency to make that move.

I recognize the difficult trade-offs we need to make as adults. The need for security and personal fulfillment can sometimes conflict with each other. I am not here to say to quit your day job because you dislike it. Nor am I here to claim that being laid off is the best thing that could happen to you. Life will be different either way, and there will be a loss involved. I am here to encourage you to stop, pause, and take stock of who you are as a person. The disruption of being laid off can make you feel like everything is out of your control, as if the universe is acting upon you and you have to cope. But there is always an element of choice—a choice not to be a victim of circumstance but to become the designer of your own life. Designing your own life involves reconciling very real needs (financial, security, social) with very real wants (fulfillment, growth, and balance) and figuring out how you can create your own path forward without waiting for others to do it for you. That choice starts by pausing and prioritizing your well-being first.

WHERE IS CLIENT B. NOW?

Today, Client B. is ready to embark on a new chapter in his life. He spent three years at a Big Five consulting firm and realized that he had learned a lot from that organization but was prepared for a change. He returned to school to earn a doctoral degree in an area he feels passionate about. He began working with private clients as a coach. He is happily married and enjoys the freedom and time to invest in his relationship. None of this would have been possible had he not taken the time to intentionally examine the fears influencing him, his choices, and what actions to take. In short, he stopped being a victim of circumstance and forged his own path forward.

Sometimes jumping in to a change or transition is a way to learn how to fly and gain your true wings. Sometimes you leap, and sometimes you are pushed. You are an expert in your life and your needs. What works today may not work tomorrow. So, trust yourself and what aligns with you. Be comfortable being yourself as you explore what comes next, both personally and professionally. Life will continue to unfold. Life isn't tidy; it's messy, and messiness can be really good.

READER ENGAGEMENT

Asking the hard questions is essential during a transition and transformation. These questions keep us moving forward. It isn't always easy to pose them or to be honest with ourselves during such times, but ultimately, you will see how this experience changes and can improve you. Take the time to explore, ask questions, be honest with yourself, and embrace the journey.

Below are questions you can ask yourself during this transition and transformation. These questions can guide you on your path.

- What kind of person do you want to be, and how do you get there?
- Are you stuck in your old narrative?
- What is your new narrative?
- What change do you want to bring to your life?
- What do you want to make, create, or build in your life?
- What gives you meaning in life?
- What can you do if your limiting beliefs are getting in your way?
- What gives you energy?
- What depletes your energy?
- What has worked well for you?
- What have been your challenges?
- What did you learn about yourself after your transition and transformation journey?

CHAPTER 7

Introspection is The Greatest Gift To Yourself

When you're working, you invest your time and energy thinking, "I'm going to be here for the next five to ten years." When that doesn't happen and someone decides your job is going away, you may feel cheated or like it was a slap in the face. You've committed yourself to this job, and now it's ending. Your life has been disrupted. You need to lean into other aspects of your life in a new, reimagined way. How scary must this feel, and how do you even go about navigating this?

Why do we only take the time for introspection when something dramatic or traumatic occurs in our lives? If we live in a society that emphasizes wellness, well-being, and mindfulness, why aren't we making introspection a regular practice? Why wait until it is forced upon us?

In this chapter, we will focus on the gift of introspection, the value it can bring to your life, and how to embrace it to move forward. You will also read Gina's story about how she embraced introspection and how it guided her through her journey from being laid off to where she is now. She approached it with vulnerability, strength, and perseverance, and didn't do it alone.

Her journey was bumpy, with unexpected moments. She wanted to share her story "so you know that you can achieve whatever dream is in your heart, no matter what obstacles you face."

INTERVIEW WITH GINA: "EMBRACING THE JOURNEY OF STARTING OVER"

It all started with an email from my boss, letting me know to stay home and await further communication. She called me to inform me that I was no longer employed, that I needed to return all my devices, and that I would receive additional instructions from HR. I hung up the phone, unable to grasp it; it was just unbelievable. I think I was in a trance. How did this happen? I've never been laid off. I have worked for twenty years without any gaps in employment and always retained a job.

After it happened, I didn't want to tell anyone. I didn't tell anyone for weeks. I have two daughters who live with me, and they knew everything that was going on, so I had to tell them. But I wasn't dating anyone at the time and all my friends live far away so I could hide away. It was panic, denial, and loss of identity all rolled into one. I was raised in a family where everything always appeared perfect on the outside. Your dirty laundry stayed inside the house, and you always put on an excellent front. My dad was always perfect, and for me, losing my job at that moment felt like the biggest failure. I've been through a lot, but that pivotal moment was when my whole world collapsed. And it wasn't just my world; it was my identity and my reputation. How do I tell the world I lost my job?

It's interesting because, as the person experiencing it, we associate a lot of shame and guilt with being laid off. I began questioning every move I had made over the past four months, trying to figure out what had gone wrong and what had transpired. I reflected on what could have happened and all my conversations, thinking I shouldn't have said this or that, just trying to make sense of the situation. So how do you fix it? How do you move forward if you're not 100% sure of what you did?

My panic and fear were weighing heavily on me. It was tough because I couldn't talk to anyone. I only had my daughters to lean on which was a lot to put on them. Thank God they're older. The day after I was laid off, I woke up with my first thought being, "I need to find a job. I'm going to do this, I'm going to find a job, and I'm going to make it so smooth that I don't have to tell anybody that I lost my job."

I was in problem-solving mode and immediately went to LinkedIn. I thought, "Okay, let me find that job," believing I could switch companies. I reviewed everyone who had ever contacted me and sent emails. Sure enough, one of the recruiters asked, "Why don't we meet on Friday?" I met the recruiter, but, unfortunately, I was completely unprepared. I hadn't researched the company, nor had I looked at the recruiter's background. I didn't even know what the position was. I was so unprepared but happy to talk to someone who could help me find a job.

I wasn't ready for this conversation, and I was mostly unprepared to discuss losing my job. I had no idea what I would say. As a result of that meeting, I had two phone interviews the following Tuesday but never heard back from them. I kept looking for a job. Three weeks went by, and I began to feel depressed. I reached a point where I started to feel the guilt, the fear, the "What did I do?" "How did I lose my job?" I felt responsible. During that time, I wasn't even placing any responsibility on them. I absorbed it all. I kept telling myself, "Okay, it's my fault I lost my job. I can't believe I did this. I'm a failure, blah blah blah." This went on for weeks, and I panicked. How was I going to pay the bills? I was confused and still hadn't accepted what had happened. Then came the realization that finding a job would be hard and take more than three weeks.

I had the opportunity to work with a career coach at an outplacement office, and that was when I began to let go of negative thoughts and open up to change. Collaborating with a career coach made me realize that the job search would take much longer than I had anticipated. However, just being in a room with others who had also been laid off was comforting. I considered myself fortunate because, when I attended, there were executives who had been with their companies for twenty-five years. I know many people, like me, feel like others can't understand or relate to their challenges. I gradually came to understand that I was not alone.

While working with my career coach and exploring all my options, I kept asking myself if I truly wanted to return to retail. I have been in retail for twenty years. As I was exploring options, I realized there was an opportunity to look beyond retail. Being in a structured environment, having support, and talking to someone helped me open my eyes to new possibilities. I began to understand why the recruiters weren't calling me back: I had not allowed myself to grieve the loss of my job. I wasn't prepared to discuss being laid off, and I didn't know what I wanted to do next; I just wasn't ready. Losing your job is a loss. I'm not used to mourning. I don't dwell on things. I'm a go-getter. I'm a problem-solver. I tried to do that but couldn't because I needed to let everything sink in.

After a lot of introspection and being open to new opportunities and ways of thinking, I reached out to a coach I admired and followed on LinkedIn. He was very bold, vulnerable, and open, which was quite different from my style because I tend to be closed off. So I contacted him and said, "Hey, I'm exploring my next job opportunity, and I'd love to learn more about what you do." I wanted to understand his perspective and gain insights into his work. He offered me a complimentary session, and I had a fantastic conversation with him. We began to dive into what had happened. I was not forgiving myself and held myself accountable in a challenging way without fully confronting the issue. I had been hiding from the world and hadn't even told my mother. The thought of revealing to her that I didn't have a job was overwhelming. I'm genuinely grateful for that conversation because I learned a lot.

The most significant piece that emerged was the loss of identity we experience when we are tied to a job. Additionally, I reflected on how hard we can be on ourselves. It took me months to accept this and let go. I considered what might have happened if they had given me a different explanation and more information. Would it have been different if I had been able to process it in another way? Possibly, but I was grappling with the fact that my once impeccable reputation was now in question. I needed clarity. It revolved around having that impeccable reputation and then watching something tarnish it in front of the world. After that coaching session, I acknowledged my feelings and understood how to move forward.

One of the things the coach challenged me on was letting the world know that I had lost my job. He asked me, "Why don't you tell the world you lost your job? Why don't you write an article?" It took me a good four or five days to figure out what to say. After I published the article, oh, my gosh, I received so many responses. I spent at least two weeks replying to messages. Recruiters reached out to me. People contacted me privately to say, "Thank you for putting this out there. I was let go, too." It was almost like a "me too" movement type of thing. Seeing the number of people and how liberating it was to share with the world that I had lost my job was wild. I could finally breathe.

INTROSPECTION: WHAT ARE YOU WAITING FOR?

Our careers reflect our education, experience, and hard work, and whether we admit it or not, they define us. After a layoff, we must undergo an emotional recovery. Whether you've recently been laid off or it has been some time since it happened, introspection should play a significant role in your recovery and reset process. You owe it to yourself to take the time to reflect. Spend time contemplating your feelings, the narrative you've constructed about being laid off, and how you wish to change that narrative. After a layoff, you've likely experienced what is referred to as an "emotional storm"—anger, shock, disbelief, and feeling shattered. It is crucial to process what has happened because your sense of self often diminishes, causing you to question everything you know about yourself. Essentially, you want to acknowledge and embrace your feelings, be honest with yourself, and choose to take action and move forward. This is where introspection, one of the best gifts you can give yourself, comes into play.

Introspection is a significant word with tremendous impact; it compels us to dive deep into ourselves in ways we might not have done before, stirring up a whole host of emotions. We need to understand introspection in this context. Introspection is an examination of your own personal mental and emotional state, a deliberate, analytical process of reflection. Most of us don't do this much, or ever, because frankly, it isn't easy, and it takes a lot of work! Introspection is very personal, thought-provoking, emotional, and, of course, scary as hell. But it needs to be done to move forward so you can create a new story and narrative for yourself.

Feeling scared is one of the most common emotions that arises in moments like this. And it's okay to feel scared. "Being scared means you're about to do something really, really brave,"[21] according to Mindy Hale. I had to include this quote in the book, specifically in this chapter, because feeling scared is part of this process, part of our introspection, healing, and moving forward. It is a powerful emotion that we all experience, especially when we are laid off and when we are trying to reimagine what our lives will look like.

As I conducted the book interviews and listened to everyone's stories, I had the honor of witnessing their raw emotions. I closely observed each person's body language, how they leaned into the conversation at different times, and the words they used to describe their experiences from the beginning of their journeys to where they found themselves on the other side. One thing I noticed in every interview was that everyone had embraced the introspective process. They incorporated it into their journeys. They created the space they needed to look in the mirror, be completely vulnerable and honest with themselves, and reflect on who they were at that moment, who they wanted to be, and how they would get there. Arianna Huffington eloquently said, "When we learn to accept ourselves—not just our public achievements and private successes but also our failures, inadequacies, cowardices, and desires—then we can transcend our fears."[22] I could not have said it better, so why not embrace this mindset and take a good look at ourselves?

There is great strength and power in being scared and even saying the words out loud, "I am scared." Is it our default to think that if we are scared of something, it means something bad or negative, or that something isn't going to work out? Are you hesitating to try something because you are scared, or does it paralyze you? We all define this differently, and it can be used interchangeably. We've all experienced moments of fear throughout our lives, and that won't stop, but what do we do with it? Why not use this powerful emotion to open your mind and heart, allowing something new, exciting, and wonderful to happen?

Why am I focusing specifically on being scared? As I worked on the book, engaged with my clients, and discussed it with friends, I noticed that this is a common issue that holds many of us back, obstructs our path, and creates barriers to genuine exploration and reflection. We often find ourselves stuck in thoughts about the past, concerning who we used to be, and when something as traumatic as a layoff or another significant event occurs, we struggle to envision what could be, what lies beyond our self-perception. Why remain stuck? Why stay paralyzed? Give yourself the greatest gift of introspection.

THE VALUE OF INTROSPECTION

When we are laid off and learn that we no longer have a job to go to, emotions overwhelm us; it becomes hard to make sense of what is happening, to separate the facts from the feelings, and we struggle to see things clearly. For any introspection to take place, we must set our emotions aside and create space to be open and vulnerable. We need to set aside our egos and be receptive to information and facts about ourselves.

When we embark on any type of introspection, we tend to ask a lot of questions, especially the "why." I get it; I am a "why" girl, and it helps me make sense of things and move forward. But if you become preoccupied with just wanting to know the "why," are you keeping yourself stuck in the past? While it may provide comfort and help us justify our experiences, we also need to reach a point where we are not only justifying what has happened but also rectifying it. Is introspection alone enough?

Through introspection, countless possibilities and new paths for self-reflection emerge. A common term for this is *mindfulness,* as it is a crucial aspect of self-introspection. Mindfulness enables us to observe our thoughts and feelings, acknowledging and accepting them without judgment. To put it more simply, it's not about fixing or changing your thoughts or emotions but about noticing and accepting them as is.

LEAN IN SO YOU CAN MOVE FORWARD

Leaning into other elements of our lives to move forward, what does this mean? When we truly lean in, we can strengthen a more well-rounded sense of ourselves. We view ourselves as whole individuals. You are more than just your job. There is so much more to who you are, who you aspire to be, and how you want others to perceive you. After a layoff, it's time to expand your horizons and reflect on yourself post-loss, so you don't get stuck in the narrative you're telling yourself about who you used to be. It's quite common to start *"shoulding"* all over yourself during a time like this. For example, "I *should* have seen this coming. I *should* have done this, or I *should* have done that." How is this helping you, and why continue to "should" all over yourself when you can move forward?

I came across a great article about *How to Get Over Losing Your Job* by Allie Volpe, which quoted Lise Obré-Austin, who said, "Sitting with and parsing your feelings is essential to moving on from the shock and anger you may be experiencing . . . Introspection can help you avoid getting defensive, which, in turn, helps you turn a setback into an opportunity for growth. We want to be able to learn any lessons about the reasons you were fired and be able to take that with you rather than place blame on former employers or partners."[23] Lauren Howe, also quoted in the article, stated, "Believing in the possibility of change is important."[24] To recognize that whatever happened, you can be a different person in the future, whether that's becoming a more sensitive romantic partner or honing different skills at work. You aren't doomed to repeat the same mistakes. As you change, your needs will change as well. Even if you just left your dream job, your definition of the perfect gig now isn't what it will be a few years down the road. And knowing that nothing stays ideal forever makes it that much easier to let go.

It's easy to dwell on the negatives, which is a common trap for many. However, it's essential to remember the positive aspects. Consider the relationships you've built, the skills you've developed, the experiences you've had, and the challenges you faced and overcame. This period allowed for personal development and growth.

You have to "clean slate" to move forward. What is "clean slating?" It is an opportunity for a fresh start, a blank canvas, to begin something new with the new version of who you want to be. It is not about bringing the old baggage and negative emotions to something new. It is unfair to bring the past into the new job and the new people you work with. What happened in your old job occurred in the past. You will only close yourself off and remain stuck if you don't "clean slate" and move forward. If you don't, you will continue to carry the old and use that story as your default, creating more obstacles that prevent you from seeing and embracing what can be. Why do all this great work on yourself—the time you took for introspection and reflection—if you plan to bring the old into the present and your future? Think about what you could be missing out on.

After being laid off and as this chapter in your life closes, consider what gives you clarity, motivates you, excites you, and energizes you. How do you want to be challenged, and how do you wish to feel valued? What will bring out the best version of yourself? It doesn't have to be just a job you focus on; there are other aspects of your life that are equally important, if not more so. As Simon Sinek says, "Always plan for the fact that no plan goes according to plan." Being laid off was not our choice, but sometimes it's a gift that we didn't realize we needed to move forward in our lives and reimagine who we can become. "Research also shows that how we bounce back from a job loss is closely related to how we process it. This "processing" is not about planning out the next steps of our careers. Rather, it's about sitting with ourselves, paying attention to our feelings, re-evaluating our learnings from past experiences, and then figuring out our next steps. This takes time, effort, and most of all, a lot of patience."[25]

You've read up to this point about what introspection is, its value and benefits, how it can impact you and others, and why you should embrace this journey. Now, let's discuss how to create and embrace this practice. Remember that these are not absolutes; these are merely recommendations, and you need to develop a practice that works for you. It is not a one-size-fits-all approach. It is about what makes sense for you and your needs.

1. It's okay not to be okay. Having an awareness of your feelings is essential to starting this process and processing the situation.

2. Accept your emotions. You will experience various emotions, sit with them, acknowledge them, and then decide how you want to move forward.

3. Diminish any personal stigma surrounding introspection. Eliminate the idea that introspection is somehow a weakness.

4. Encourage vulnerability. Be open and honest with yourself, ask difficult questions, and understand that vulnerability is not a weakness. In that moment, you are truly being brave and courageous.

5. Allow yourself grace and kindness during this time. Reach out for help because you shouldn't navigate this process alone. Let others in and allow them to support you.

6. Find the time for introspection. Embrace this process. Pay attention to what your mind, body, and heart are telling you.

7. Recognize that this process can be challenging. It requires time and varies for each person.

8. Don't get stuck in the "what-ifs." This will hold you back and may create obstacles to moving forward. It will keep you focused on the past and your old narrative.

9. Engage with your community. If you lack one,

create one. Surrounding yourself with others will help you feel supported and less isolated. Form a community that fulfills your needs.

10. Reflect on who you are, what you want, and what is possible. This will help you start reimagining your identity and move forward. It will enable you to stay present and consider what can be instead of what was.

11. Find an outlet to express your feelings. This can be a journaling practice, art, dance, a support group, or anything you need to articulate your emotions instead of keeping them to yourself.

12. Most of all, *trust yourself!*

13. You will be okay.

REVISITING GINA

I did a tremendous amount of introspection. I am a different person today than I was then. I've learned so much about myself and my gifts, embracing my identity beyond my career. There is so much more to who I am. However, I didn't reach this point on my own; I had a lot of coaching. To get there, you must step outside of yourself, take a holistic look, and ask, "Okay, wait a minute, what's going on here?" Then, you realize, "Oh, yeah, I gave myself to this job." Recognize what's important to you, what your values are, the legacy you want to leave, and the life you want to live.

When something disruptive and traumatic happens, no matter what the transition is, you have to examine all areas of your life. Being laid off compelled me to reflect on my life and my identity. I used to be someone who believed that as long as my work life was thriving, I could manage the chaos in every other aspect of my life. I spent many years living an unbalanced life. It wasn't until that moment and during that transformation that I realized that's not the way to live.

Many of us associate being laid off with failure. But it's not a failure; it was a tremendous opportunity to learn, grow, and refocus my life. It was a time to pause and ask myself, "What's important? What do I want to do? What is the impact I'm having in my life?" I think we need to rethink how we define failure, especially regarding our support system. Understand that you're not alone, that there's an opportunity, and build a support system. You can't hide from it; you must embrace it. You need to have people around you. I also didn't want anyone's pity. I realized that by being selective about the support system I created, I wouldn't receive pity. Instead, I would get the support and understanding I needed. I surrounded myself with people who challenged me to see things differently.

There is so much I've learned about myself, and I'm going to share two key takeaways. First, it's important to balance all aspects of my life. This realization helped me see that I wasn't pursuing my dreams and that I wasn't involved in the community. I didn't incorporate all the things that mattered to me into my life. Second, I think about myself, and what I mean by that is it's okay not to be perfect, and it's fine to be vulnerable. Am I the best version of myself for where I am now? Yes, I'm the best version of myself in this moment, but I know there's much more work ahead to reach the next version. After this transformation, I'm more aware of when I'm not living my true life. There's a heightened awareness of who I want to be and how I want to show up, so when I'm not, I think, "Wait a minute, I'm not walking the talk."

WHERE IS GINA NOW?

It was hard for Gina to accept that after twenty years of building a fantastic career in retail, she lost her job. Today, Gina is the founder of her own coaching business and serves as an Executive Leadership and High-Performance Coach. She has learned to find harmony and balance in her personal and professional life, which she once thought was impossible.

In early 2021, Gina faced the most challenging time of her life. She was in perfect health when she was diagnosed with breast cancer out of nowhere. Her priorities shifted, and she began a second transformational journey that included crucial health, financial, and business decisions.

After a fourteen-month journey of treatment and healing, Gina feels even more inspired and determined to help others succeed and broaden her impact on the world.

READER ENGAGEMENT

I hope that after reading this chapter, you will leave with a clearer understanding of why introspection is a gift you should give yourself—not only when something happens in your life but also as a regular part of mindfulness, wellness, and well-being. You will recognize its tremendous value and lasting benefits. You can begin your introspection journey by reflecting on the following questions. Maintain this as an ongoing practice, not just a one-time effort.

- Have you ever taken a moment for introspection without being prompted by an experience, incident, or traumatic event?

- What value did you find from your introspection journey?
- Have you considered incorporating introspection into a regular lifestyle practice instead of only doing it when something is happening?
- How can you incorporate introspection into a regular practice of mindfulness, wellness, and well-being?
- If you have undergone a journey of introspection, what advice would you offer someone about introspection?

CHAPTER 8

Are You Just Your Job?

What do you want others to know about you when you first meet them, and how do you want to be remembered? We spend so much time figuring out who we are and how to showcase that. However, when we define our identity, purpose, and beliefs through a single lens, are we misrepresenting them and placing them in the wrong context? What I mean is, are you prioritizing your professional identity above everything else? Our identity reflects our individual uniqueness; it isn't just one thing; it is multifaceted. We don't want to be known solely by a label tied to our profession or workplace. There is so much more to who we are, and don't you want people to see the complete you, not just one part? Does linking your identity to your career give you more agency, or does it limit you?

When will we stop shaping our lives around our jobs and instead find a way to incorporate our jobs into our lives? For many of us, life is centered around work. When we experience a layoff, we often feel immense shock, uncertainty, and fear, leading us to question everything about our identities. We tend to measure our worth, purpose, abilities, and sense of self by our jobs. It's important to recognize that a job should reflect more than just your value.

Do you struggle to let go of the past and who you once were? Are you trapped in the narrative of your former identity? How are you redefining your sense of self? What does job loss signify for you, and what implications does it carry for your future? When you've been laid off, it presents an opportunity to separate your identity from your job and create a new narrative that encompasses your whole self, not just your professional role. In this chapter, we will delve into all the questions mentioned above. You will read my interview with Holly, who went through an identity crisis after losing her job. Finally, we will discuss how to reshape your identity, design your career around your life, why you should avoid defining yourself by your job, and what steps to take next.

Holly was referred to me through an employer-sponsored support program. When we began working together, she had recently been laid off from a "Big Five" publishing company. She came to me for help in dealing with the emotional fallout from her job loss and establishing her business. Holly was already quite advanced in processing her emotions with a therapist and had started the initial stages of setting up her business, which is somewhat unusual compared to my other clients. I immediately sensed that she had great energy and was highly motivated. She was eager to take the leap and explore what her business could mean for her clients, family, and herself. One notable aspect of her experience is how she thoroughly examined the issues surrounding her identity and transformation.

INTERVIEW WITH HOLLY: "THE BEST THING I DIDN'T KNOW I WANTED"

I sensed that being laid off was imminent. There had already been two rounds of layoffs in the past year, and I became part of the third. We had a new president who made it clear that one of his goals was to reduce headcount. We all felt somewhat dispensable. The warning signs for me were that I suddenly wasn't receiving responses to my emails, or the replies had a different tone and sometimes seemed delayed. A high-profile project came in about a week before I was let go, and I was very excited about it. I sent it to my publisher, who had always supported me. She was like a mentor to me. However, I didn't hear anything back, which felt quite odd. Still, she continued to provide me with affirmations. The day before our weekly editorial meeting, she reached out at 6:00 a.m., telling me she didn't think the project was right for us and that she didn't want me to bring it up in the meeting. I sensed something was off.

By chance, I had a session with my therapist that day during my lunch break. I told her, "I think I'm being let go." We discussed all the signs and signals. Maybe it was just a coincidence that these things were happening. She then asked, "Okay, what if this does happen? How will you react?" We talked about it enough that when it did happen, I felt more prepared than I had anticipated the day before.

Here's how it all happened. I received a call from my direct supervisor to meet with her in her office. It was 4:15 p.m., and she asked me to sit down. She told me to close the door, and I thought, "Well, that's that," because we never closed the door. She then said, "I don't know how else to say this, but your position has been eliminated." I was really proud of myself for not crying. However, at that moment, I felt a surge of anger. I wasn't happy about it at all; it certainly wasn't closure, but simply knowing for sure had a somewhat settling effect.

I asked her if she needed anything else from me, when my last day would be, who was taking over my books, and what was happening to my assistant. At that time, she was only assisting me and was new to the role, but she still shouldn't be collateral damage. They already had a plan for her; they assigned her to someone else's desk. Then, I returned to my desk and received a call from HR asking if I had time to pick up the paperwork.

It was incredibly sad. There was a cheerful sunshine-yellow folder with my name on it and inside were all my severance papers. I spoke briefly with the HR representative and collected the documents. My closest colleague and I went out for drinks, and then I cried. I was still in shock and very angry, but she just let me talk. She was angry both with me and on my behalf, and she was amazing.

They let me go on February 1, and my last day was March 1. In retrospect, that felt like a long time and could have been shorter. However, I appreciated that they extended it to March so my health insurance remained effective through that month. I received a decent severance for my ten years with the company. They compensated me with two weeks of pay for each year I worked, totaling about six months of salary. They also covered my COBRA for six months, which was great since my family's insurance was through me.

The next day, my publisher entered my office, something she had never done before. She sank into the chair across from my desk and said, "I just want you to know this wasn't personal. I like and respect you so much. I believe you have tremendous potential." I replied, "Yeah, but you still let me go, and I still don't have a job." Everyone kept reiterating that it wasn't personal, but it felt profoundly personal to me. I understood why my position was eliminated. I was low enough on the totem pole, didn't earn much, and had an assistant. Someone else made the decision to let me go, which was the difficult part; my lack of control was probably the hardest aspect for me because I don't make decisions lightly.

Another difficult aspect was that my whole identity was tied to my job. I was an editor at one of the Big Five publishing houses in New York City. I worked in a historic building with an office that had a door and a window—a dream come true. I had worked so hard for so long to reach that point. I know I'm other things, but having that taken away from me without another job lined up was jarring. I never considered myself anything other than a publishing house employee. It never crossed my mind to pursue anything else. After all, I never would have thought to leave my job to start my own business or anything like that in a million years. It was always, "I will be an editor at a publishing house until I retire. Hopefully, the same one, but I can explore other opportunities, and it'll be fine."

Before I was laid off, I had started searching for other jobs but couldn't find anything appealing to pursue. I can't remember how the idea of starting my own editorial business came about. But as soon as it was said aloud, I thought, "Yeah, that's what I'm going to do." And I ran with it. I registered my LLC while I was still at my job. I was so angry, and nothing fueled my passion more than pure rage. I thought, "I am going to show them. I am going to do this." It wasn't until I had left the building for the last time that I felt the weight lift off my shoulders. I realized this was no longer my problem, and I could finally take a deep breath again.

I spent several days organizing my house and tackling tasks I had overlooked for too long. I worked on developing my service list and rate sheet, and I even started discussing my website with others. I had no idea what I was doing since I lacked a business background. It required a great deal of research and learning, but I felt genuinely excited. I asked a lot of questions about starting my business. I didn't want another job; this was what I truly desired. I knew I had something people would pay for—my expertise and extensive background in publishing. The information I can provide to authors is invaluable.

I built my business from my kitchen counter, the couch, and Starbucks. Isn't it amazing what you can accomplish when you're happy and no longer have to commute into the city? So much good has come from being laid off. I feel more engaged in my life. When I was working in the city and commuting, I felt like I wasn't a good employee, mom, or wife. I struggled to hold it all together, but I don't feel that way anymore. If my business needs a little more time and attention, that's okay. I know the kids will be fine, and I am there for them. I can shift the balance where it's needed.

I received a solid severance package and had six months to determine whether this business would be viable. I used that time to assess if I could turn a profit, whether this venture had potential, or if I needed to seek a corporate job. Not everyone has the opportunity to take that time to experiment. I was fortunate, and that's why I wouldn't have pursued this path if I hadn't been laid off. I would never have just said, "Screw you guys. I'm starting my own business. Peace out." For my life and personality, being laid off pushed me in a direction that ultimately turned out to be the best thing ever.

MY TRANSITION AND TRANSFORMATION

"I am not my job." Let me repeat that: "I am not my job." This was the most important lesson I had to learn. I am much more than just my job title, past or present. It took me a whole year to come to terms with being laid off. I found the closure I didn't know I needed. I could shape how the process unfolded. I had control over my environment. I could show up the way I wanted and be as present as I chose to be.

We need to examine how we approach work and our careers with a fresh mindset and perspective. Success should be defined by how you thrive in life, not just by your professional achievements. After losing that aspect of my identity, I realized that our jobs shouldn't encompass the entirety of who we are. Instead, we should focus on our happiness and what else brings fulfillment to our lives.

A CHANGE IN IDENTITY

One thing that really stands out about Holly's story is what she mentioned about her identity. To paraphrase that interview, I want you to understand that you are not defined by your job. Let me emphasize that again: *you are not your job*. Your job does not define who you are. You may not believe this yet. It takes time, but one day you'll genuinely internalize that message. The key is to start that process early and consistently reinforce it with yourself, even when society makes it difficult.

Have you ever noticed that when you first meet someone, the initial question often asked is, "What do you do, or who do you work for?" Why do we begin conversations with this inquiry instead of asking what they enjoy or how they spend their free time? The reality is that work plays a significant role in our lives; it is linked to our income and security and can offer a sense of purpose and fulfillment. Don't get me wrong; there's nothing wrong with working hard, loving what you do, or identifying with your job. However, the problem arises when you identify too closely with your work, losing sight of other important aspects of your life. Many of us have intertwined our entire identities with our jobs, our titles, the companies we work for, or our salaries. This is what we need to avoid. But what happens when, one day, you are told, "I am sorry, but your position has been eliminated, and we have to let you go." What becomes of your identity then?

Who are you at that point? You could genuinely find yourself in an identity crisis.

We all appreciate, or even require, recognition, praise, or prestige for our work. We base our self-worth on this, but it becomes problematic when we rely on it too much, causing other areas of our lives to become blurred. Psychologists use the term 'enmeshment' to describe a situation where the boundaries between individuals become unclear, leading individual identities to lose significance. Enmeshment hinders the development of a stable, independent sense of self.[26]

Understanding how we reached this point is important, as we've invested much of our adult lives in developing our skills, building our reputation, shaping our identity, earning money, and reflecting on how our careers define us. This isn't just about our self-image; it's also about how we gauge ourselves in relation to others. When we know where someone works, their title, and similar details, we can evaluate the competitive landscape and the dynamics of our relationships. We might not do this consciously, or perhaps we do. If this is our standard for self-assessment, how can we avoid judging others in the same way?

If we consider how our families, society, and colleagues perceive us based on our work achievements and salary as indicators of our accomplishments and status, how can we avoid tying our identity to what we do, and at what cost? It's no surprise that this has happened to many of us because we live in a culture that supports and even promotes it. How do you spend most of your time during the day and week? Do you have hobbies or interests outside of work, or are you too busy to pursue them because of your workload? What justifications do you make for this choice?

Perhaps it is because we lack a clear understanding of who we are outside of work. Do we truly know ourselves as we ought to? Consider this: if someone asks you to describe yourself using a list of adjectives, I bet you start that list with how you think others perceive you in relation to your career, and then you might follow with other words that reflect your personality, character, or values. Why don't we prioritize our identities beyond our jobs or careers?

PRIORITIZING YOURSELF OVER YOUR JOB

For many, there is a sense of guilt associated with prioritizing ourselves over our jobs or other responsibilities. When we place our work above our physical, mental, and emotional well-being, it becomes a recipe for burnout. You might not even realize you were heading toward burnout before your layoff, and you may continue to feel it even afterward. Being between jobs, this could be the perfect opportunity to rediscover yourself and find a new equilibrium that will help you navigate your layoff and any new position you may encounter.

I came across an article in Harvard Business Review by Donna McGeorge, a best-selling author and global authority on productivity. She shares that, "Despite the demands of an ever-changing world, one thing is clear: Taking care of your health, regardless of what the culture tells you, is critical to your growth and success. You don't have to prove yourself before prioritizing yourself. In fact, the opposite is true: You need to prioritize yourself to perform at your best. The earlier you start to build healthy habits, the happier and more fulfilled you will be."[27]

McGeorge recommends four things to help you prioritize yourself over your job:

1.   Build in time to do nothing.
2.   Learn to say "No."
3.   Keep your work and life separate.
4.   Understand what work really means to you.

These are excellent tips from McGeorge about prioritizing yourself overall, but let's examine how to apply them to life after being laid off. Let's break down the four tips suggested earlier.

- **Build in time to do nothing:** You may feel an urgency to find a job immediately and even guilt for not job searching while engaging in other activities, even briefly. However, by taking breaks, you give yourself a chance to rest, recharge, and refocus, allowing your mind and body to recuperate. Although you might need to secure employment quickly for financial reasons, it's crucial to set aside time for yourself. If you have some flexibility due to savings or a severance package, this becomes even more important. Use this time to fully rest and recuperate. Give yourself the space to unwind. Explore new self-care techniques and find ways to better manage stress. This approach can also help prevent burnout in future jobs.

- **Learn to say no:** How many of you feel guilty about saying no? Is there a fear of missing out on something, or are you worried about upsetting someone? After being laid off, it can be tempting to accept every networking opportunity. However, it's important to incorporate the word "no" into your vocabulary and to decline events or anything else that brings stress or uncertainty into your life. Center your activities around yourself and your family and focus on what you need right now. You will feel much better when you do.

- **Keep your work and personal life separate:** Allowing work to seep into other areas of your life can lead to burnout and reduced productivity. What steps can you take to address this, and how can you cultivate healthy habits for yourself? There are several strategies to consider, ranging from your physical space to your mental health. Let's start with your physical environment.

  If possible, establish a designated workspace where you can concentrate solely on work, whatever that may be, and avoid taking your laptop to bed. For job seekers in this situation, look for a workspace outside your home if you can. This could be a local café, a coworking space, the library, or any place that suits you. Consider spending a few hours there each day or a few days a week. You will appreciate the change of scenery, as a different environment can provide you with energy and motivation, and you never know whom you might encounter. It is also essential to maintain a schedule and set boundaries regarding when you will start and stop working for the day.

Next, consider the mental health aspects of separating work from personal life. Prioritize your personal life—family, friends, and, most importantly, your self-care. Make sure that in conversations, you aren't always discussing work. Explore new hobbies. Read a book. Essentially, take an interest in other aspects of your life, whatever they may be.

- **Understand what work truly means to you:** This will evolve throughout your life. Let's focus on your current circumstances. Ask yourself, "What does work mean to me? Why is this important?" Take this chance to reflect on how much of your life is influenced by your job compared to other aspects. Consider, "Who am I outside of work?" Envision how your life can look and what you want to approach differently in your work moving forward. Our default mindset when contemplating what work signifies often centers around salary, security, stability, and purpose. Others may express that it's about serving others, helping individuals, leading, and participating in something larger than themselves.

Reflecting on these tough questions and being truly honest will help you find the right path for your life and your current circumstances. However, never forget that there is much more to our lives than just work. Don't lose sight of your core values and beliefs and how they align with your life, as they help shape a strong identity that isn't merely dependent on one aspect. Are you shaping your life around your job, or are you shaping your job around your life?

BUILDING YOUR JOB AROUND YOUR LIFE

Are you shaping your life around your job, or your job around your life? Have you taken a moment to consider all the areas of your life and where you stand in each of them? I'm referring to self-care, career, relationships, community, parenting and family, spirituality, health, personal growth and development, and finances, to name a few. By ranking them in order of importance, you can gain a clearer perspective on where your life currently stands, what direction it's heading, and where you want it to go.

When I work with a client experiencing an identity crisis after being laid off, where their self-worth is entirely tied to their job, I prefer to have them partake in a reality check exercise that encourages reflection on their current life outside of work. This exercise is essentially a modified form of a gap analysis. For those unfamiliar with the term, gap analysis is used in business to evaluate performance against desired outcomes. In this context, it helps assess one's present and future life and identify what matters most to them. Consequently, individuals can formulate a plan to address areas in their lives that are lacking or that they wish to improve. Below are the nine areas mentioned earlier. These are the ones I typically start with, but you can add or adjust them as needed. Essentially, you create this based on different aspects of your life. It's also beneficial to revisit this periodically to evaluate your progress.

Topic	Current State	Gap	Future State (Desired Outcome)
Self-care	I am not making enough time during the week to exercise because I am working too much.	I am only making time once a week, during the weekend, to exercise.	I would like to make time 3x a week to exercise.
Career			
Relationships			
Community			
Parenting/ Family			
Spirituality			
Health			
Personal Growth & Development			
Finances			

We need to reframe our relationship with both our careers and ourselves, recognizing that life extends beyond just work. Don't get me wrong; being connected to your job and career is incredibly important, but it's not everything. This means reclaiming your time and identity, engaging more in activities and relationships, and achieving that balance in your life—the life you desire, not merely what you feel you must do, whether self-imposed or dictated by others.

Full transparency here: I have been where you are now. I was that person whose entire identity was tied to what I did for a living. Now, in my second career, I have rebranded and reimagined my life by finding something I love. However, since I own my business, I've had to be careful not to link everything to my career. I must admit that it's a work in progress every day, and I am constantly learning how to improve in this area. Some days are harder than others. During the pandemic, I had an excuse; I couldn't do anything else, which made it easy to connect everything to my work. But now that we have come out of the pandemic, I can't use that as an excuse anymore, nor do I want to. I want to be recognized for more than just my job because there is so much more to my life and who I am. That's what I want for you, and what you should desire for yourself.

WHAT TO DO NEXT

As you've been reading throughout this chapter, you understand why we tie our identity to our jobs. We live in a culture that promotes this, and we make excuses to justify it to ourselves and to others. We recognize the damage it causes because we're experiencing it, and for many, this is all we know. If you have been laid off, are facing an identity crisis, and can relate to any of this, let's begin by discussing why you shouldn't define yourself by your career. Then, we can take steps to move forward.

1. Having a well-known job isn't the only measure of your success.
2. Our truths and values are the only things that should define us.
3. Most jobs are temporary and can change at any moment.
4. Your job is what you do, not who you are.
5. Other people won't remember you for the job you have but for how you make them feel.

What should we do when we identify too closely with our work and overlook other important aspects of our lives? Much of this stems from the narrative we have constructed for ourselves and the version we are currently living. How can you tell the story of who you are and describe your life beyond your job when you are unsure of what that looks like?

After a layoff and as this chapter of your life concludes, you must untangle your past and present selves. Your past narrative is part of you, and you shouldn't forget it. Connecting both narratives to create a new one is beneficial. Embracing this uncertainty is essential. It's time to reimagine a new version of yourself and who you want to become.

Start with small steps. We can begin by changing the language we use to describe ourselves. Instead of starting with what you do, emphasize who you are as a person—your defining characteristics, important values, and the hobbies or activities you enjoy (not work)—and only then mention your job. You need to determine what matters to you, as you are the only one who can make this change. Consider shifting your perspective on your career, viewing yourself as a whole person and, most importantly, allowing others to see the real you.

REVISITING HOLLY

Many editors I know who have gone freelance have reached out to me because I've been very open and honest about my experiences. I inform everyone that if they have questions, they should feel free to contact me; I will answer anything I can because people did that for me, and I want to pay it forward, knowing how much it helped me. I contacted a couple of colleagues who had transitioned to freelance work to learn from their experiences and see how they managed their businesses, including what they liked and didn't like about it. If you make all your decisions in a tiny box, all by yourself, you miss the bigger picture and fail to tap into the potential out there, as you can learn from others every day if you allow yourself. Many people become stuck in their own thoughts and beliefs. This applies to all aspects of life, not just careers. You must engage with others and expand your perspective to gain valuable insights. I didn't come up with the idea of having a freelance career on my own. Someone introduced it to me, and it completely changed my perspective; it was my "ah-hah" moment, and it transformed my entire world. I feel truly grateful for being laid off. It took me a full year to realize that everything would be alright. And guess what? It is alright; it's even better than alright—it's amazing.

WHERE IS HOLLY NOW?

After being laid off, Holly's entire perspective on work shifted.

She spent four years as a freelance editor, building her business. Her success allowed her to focus on her family, prioritize her mental health, and work with clients on her own terms. That flexibility proved to be exactly what she needed during that time in her life and for her family. It enabled her to recover from the burnout she had experienced in her previous job. As she approached her fifth year, she had the opportunity to return to work at a small, independent publisher, but this time with a healthier work-life balance and greater control over her boundaries.

READER ENGAGEMENT

I suggest taking one question at a time, reflecting on it, and observing how it resonates with you. Use your understanding of how you process information, reflect, and learn to carve your own path in answering these questions.

- What percentage of your identity is your career?
- How does your career define who you are?
- What do you talk about outside of work?
- What are your hobbies outside of work, and what activities do you enjoy doing?
- What values and characteristics about yourself are important to you?
- How do you want to redefine your identity and create a new narrative about who you are?
- What version of you do you want other people to see?

CHAPTER 9

"Laid Off" Aren't Bad Words

I've been laid off, you've been laid off, you know someone who has been laid off, or you've had to let someone go, so let's talk about it. Let's discuss this openly, without shame, guilt, embarrassment, or judgment, regarding a topic that should be part of any job or career, so we don't feel bad discussing it.

We don't enter a job expecting to be laid off, so we don't prepare for it. Typically, we don't think it will happen to us. However, the past three and a half years have revealed a different reality about what is occurring. Our perceptions, realities, and fears have all shifted, and we are uncertain about where the path will lead us or when we will feel less impact from layoffs.

By the time you've reach this point, you should recognize that we can and must eliminate the shame, guilt, embarrassment, and judgment associated with being laid off. It's time to promote change and build a community based on compassion, understanding, and support. In this chapter, we will discuss changing the conversation around layoffs, conducting layoffs with compassion, and eliminating self-imposed pressures and labels connected to being laid off. This chapter highlights how we can move forward, the actions we can take, and how we can shift our perspectives and language while also reflecting on ourselves and how we think about and treat others. This is about coming together to create change.

All the interviews you've read about so far focus on individuals who have been laid off, detailing their transitions, transformations, and how they navigated their layoff journeys. However, the interview in this chapter is different. I met Bryant during my weekly career coaching group in 2020. He wasn't in the group because he had been laid off; instead, he decided to leave his job. I admire his courage to resign from a position that he recognized wasn't the right fit for him, didn't align with his core values, and didn't provide a path for growth.

After getting to know him and hearing his story, I wanted to conduct an interview with him from a different perspective because we need to see all sides of the layoff process and its impact to change how we approach it, discuss it, and eliminate the stigma associated with it. Bryant has experienced both being laid off and laying people off, and because of his experiences, he speaks about these situations with heart and compassion while offering valuable suggestions on how to treat those going through this. We know it is difficult for both sides—the ones conducting the layoffs and those being laid off—but we can change the conversation, and we can all participate in this transformation.

INTERVIEW WITH BRYANT: "WHAT'S BROKEN AND HOW TO FIX IT"

I spent nearly twenty years in Fortune 50 companies working in marketing and brand management. I appreciated the stability in those organizations and learned to navigate the Byzantine bureaucracy to make things happen, launch products, and promote disruptive ideas. However, I eventually grew weary of overseeing declines. Therefore, when the opportunity arose to work in the cannabis sector, it was exhilarating because, as a marketer, there is no greater challenge than establishing oneself in a new industry. There wasn't much noteworthy professional brand-building. So I began working at what I considered to be one of the better-run companies in the field. Initially, it was fantastic. It was incredibly exciting. Transitioning from a Fortune 50 to a start-up was wild. The industry is chaotic, but it's a type of chaos that I enjoy.

When you're working with a start-up and the company founder, chemistry and personality are crucial. In a Fortune 50 company, if you don't like or get along with the CEO, it's irrelevant because you don't have as much direct exposure to the leadership in your daily routine. Not so with a start-up. One thing I quickly recognized was that the CEO was not battle-tested. When things went wrong or the board asked tough questions, he didn't know how to handle them. There was also a level of unspoken trust among the leaders which created a really strange situation; even though I was on the leadership team, I realized I would never be part of that inner circle, which eventually became problematic.

The last six months I spent there were a terrible experience. I was miserable. I was hired for a specific job—to build the brand—but many of the company's activities hindered my ability to do that. I faced a choice: I could either put my head down and tough it out for the next year or so, but that would mean another year without anything to show for my efforts in the organization or the industry. That might have been acceptable if I were twenty-two, but I wasn't; in marketing, you're only as good as what you did last week. Even with a great track record of success, they'll look at you and say, "So what have you done lately? What have you accomplished recently?" Marketing changes so quickly and is constantly evolving. I knew I couldn't afford to take that time from my career and sit on my hands. So I negotiated my exit with the CEO.

I chose to leave that position based on several factors. I was tired of my unproductive relationship with the CEO and felt excluded from the inner circle. I could have managed these two issues if I had the runway to achieve my objectives. But if I'd stayed, I would have not only continued to face hostility from the CEO and others, but I also wouldn't have anything to show for it, nor would I be able to reach my goals. In my conversation with my boss as I was leaving, I said, "If you believe we can change, then I would love to stay and help build the company with you. Otherwise, we can amicably part ways." It took a lot of courage to have such a frank conversation, not knowing if I would leave after being fired or with the opportunity for a constructive discussion. It became clear to me that there was no winning in that conversation. It became an easy decision to say, "Okay, if that's the case, let's just discuss the numbers on what it will take for me to leave."

It was about having the clarity to understand what was broken and what it would take to fix it. People encounter various issues in their jobs for different reasons, such as a bad boss or feeling stuck. Sometimes, there's a sense of malaise without understanding why, thinking, "Why am I unhappy?" This can make it difficult to address any problems. However, I believe the first step is to ask, "What's broken? And if it can be fixed, what can I do to help fix it?" Some people work for a career, while others work for a paycheck. We've all experienced that and gone through different phases in our careers when we think, "I just need to focus on earning a paycheck right now."

If you have stayed at a job where you felt miserable for three and a half years, the most important question to ask yourself is, "Why am I feeling miserable, and can I do anything to change that now?" If one of the factors you can't change lies within the organization, can you make a change externally? Can you take on a side gig? Can you find the fulfillment you're seeking elsewhere? Address the issues connected to what is broken.

CHANGING THE CONVERSATION

Navigating a career is challenging; interviewing, accepting a job, staying employed, and leaving for any reason are emotional, transformative, and significant processes in our lives since we spend so much time working. During college, there is a strong emphasis on securing a job and building a career. So why aren't we incorporating discussions about being laid off when we begin conversations about landing our first job? If we start these discussions early and confront the realities of being laid off at a young age, we can handle these conversations more effectively, set realistic expectations, and reduce the stigma surrounding this topic. Something needs to change. I would much rather be prepared for situations like this so that I can manage my expectations and plan my actions accordingly.

Why haven't companies handled the layoff conversation effectively, and why do so many continue to struggle with it? We all have the opportunity to learn from the experiences of individuals and organizations over the past several years, and we have the potential for significant transformation. How do we change our language, perceptions, and approach to layoffs while creating a safe space for compassionate discussions about them? Specifically, how can we shift the conversation surrounding layoffs? What does it truly mean, and how can we navigate through it? How do we integrate discussions about layoffs into our mainstream conversations, just as we do when discussing job seeking and our careers?

As I conducted the interviews for this book, I consistently asked the following questions: "How can we transform the conversation about being laid off to make it part of our mainstream dialogue and reshape the perception of what it means to be laid off?" Some suggestions seem clear and straightforward, yet for some reason, this still isn't happening. Here are some examples of how we can shift the dialogue and genuinely engage in the conversation:

- Introduce the concept of layoffs to college students as they prepare to enter the workforce. Clarify that while a layoff is a possibility, it doesn't mean it will necessarily happen; it's simply a potential scenario they should acknowledge and be prepared for.
- Incorporate the conversation about layoffs in both the interview and onboarding processes. While it's unlikely to occur, it always remains a possibility. People value the transparency regarding how the company managed past layoffs and treated those affected.
- Ensure that the employee handbook includes a layoff policy and benefits package.
- Foster a culture of acceptance, free from judgment, and to encourage openness about layoffs.
- Company Communications: If layoffs are a possibility, the company—particularly its leadership, managers, and HR—needs to communicate its message clearly. The worst thing

a company can do is fail to be transparent, ignore the situation, and fail to provide support for those directly affected as well as for those who remain. Communication should explain why the layoffs are happening, how the decision was made, how those impacted will be supported, how those who stay will be assisted, and what the next steps will be. Essentially, it should convey the company's commitment to reassuring everyone that they are valued, emphasizing that human capital is the most critical aspect, and it's not just about profit.

- Create a space for open discussion. Amplifying our voices is the best way to convey that it's okay to talk about being laid off. It is *not* the fault of the person laid off, and they should not feel ashamed, guilty, or embarrassed about what occurred.

WHAT TO SAY AND WHAT NOT TO SAY

When someone tells us they have been laid off, it's important to pay attention to their words, body language, and emotions. All these factors can help us navigate the conversation. If someone feels safe discussing their layoff, they will be more open about it. However, at times, they just need someone to listen and create a safe space for them. These conversations differ in a professional setting compared to a more personal one. The tone of the conversation completely shifts if any sense of judgment is present. The individual experiencing this already feels a great deal of shame, guilt, embarrassment, and significant internal judgment.

So who is responsible for changing the conversation? Prospective employees, companies, and those laid off all provide valuable perspectives on this issue. Essentially, all of us play a role and have a voice in this matter. It will take all of us to create change, transform our language, and eliminate this problem.

Here's a suggestion on changing our language and beginning the conversation if you've been laid off: instead of saying, "I was laid off," you might say, "My old company went through a reorganization and leadership change, which led to layoffs, resulting in my role being eliminated." This clarifies that you weren't singled out, that you weren't dismissed for cause, and, most importantly, it depersonalizes the conversation. Once I changed my narrative about being laid off, it removed the shame and guilt, making me feel more comfortable discussing what happened. I had to understand it first and accept that it wasn't due to anything I did but simply something that occurred.

The world of work has dramatically changed since the pandemic, presenting us with opportunities to learn from it, evolve, adapt, and modify. Considering the number of mass layoffs occurring simultaneously, it seems implausible that all these individuals were let go for cause or had done something wrong. The landscape of work and layoffs has changed and will continue to evolve, so we must adapt. To shift the conversation around layoffs, we must create space and opportunities for these discussions. This begins with awareness, community, open conversations, empathy, learning, and growth.

LAYOFFS, THE COMPASSIONATE WAY

The way in which layoffs are conducted can influence how we discuss the experience of being laid off. We acknowledge that layoffs are an unfortunate and unavoidable reality. Regardless of how a layoff is carried out, no job can or should define your entire identity. That said, we should recognize that companies must improve their approach to these situations and need to demand it from them. This has been a recurring theme throughout the book, a point I feel strongly about and cannot emphasize enough.

If we know that layoffs will continue to occur in large numbers and at a rapid pace, what can we learn from their execution, and how can we manage the process more compassionately? This is our opportunity to recognize that there can be a caring approach to changing someone's life. We can learn from the harm we experienced in our own layoffs, and from those we've survived. It is time to unite, build a compassionate community, and support each other, as well as companies and organizations, as much as we can, both internally and externally. We cannot prevent layoffs, but we can strive for a more human-centric approach. People should be treated as individuals, not as mere resources.

As Aaron Rubens points out, "What do compassionate layoffs entail? Compassionate layoffs place the employees—rather than the company—at the forefront by addressing the mental, emotional, social, and physical needs of those affected when an organization is compelled to implement layoffs. Prioritizing people has a cascading positive impact on the entire business and can ultimately enhance the company's future. Managing your layoffs with compassion can reduce losses and protect the company's culture and brand from significant damage. When devising a compassionate strategy for layoffs, it is essential that this sentiment originates from the top, involving the CEO and leadership team. Employees must hear not only from their managers but also from top company executives, demonstrating genuine empathy during the layoff process."[28]

Much of this comes from a top-down philosophy that fosters a culture of support for those affected, emphasizing empathy and non-judgmental assistance. It is crucial for leaders to communicate clearly, ensuring full transparency and acknowledging that layoffs are the company's responsibility, not the employees'. Most importantly, companies must shift and participate in these discussions. Layoffs should be seen as part of the employee lifecycle, with plans in place to address them. Everyone needs to be involved; we must listen and communicate openly with one another. These conversations are vital.

NO SHAME, NO GUILT, AND NO JUDGMENT

I thought it was a great opportunity to start this section with a quote from Brene Brown talking about shame from her book *Daring Greatly*. She began her chapter, "Understanding and Combating Shame," in a highly actionable way. I feel like she gave us permission to let go of our shame about being laid off and to speak up for ourselves. She wrote, "Shame derives its power from being unspeakable. That's why it loves perfectionists—it's easy to keep us quiet. If we cultivate enough awareness about shame to name it and speak to it, we've basically cut it off at the knees. Shame hates having words wrapped about it. If we speak shame, it begins to wither."[29] This is our opportunity to redefine our perception of being laid off. It allows us to release the negative thoughts we carry, such as self-doubt, shame, guilt, embarrassment, and judgment. We find ourselves trapped in a continuous loop where the same negative narratives about ourselves replay repeatedly in our minds. Initially, we feel stuck in this loop and are uncertain about how to break free. We cling to what we know and what feels familiar as a way to cope with and navigate through traumatic experiences. The judgment we face when laid off often stems from this internal critique of ourselves. We worry excessively about what others will think, how they will behave around us, and what they might say or refrain from saying. We are overly concerned about the perception we believe others have of someone who has been laid off. A client once remarked that after losing her job, she felt as if she were "sitting in a stadium of judgment and didn't know how to escape."

I came across a great article by Leslie Kleinberg Zacks, who started by writing, "Dump your shame and move on." The article might be strong in tone, but there is truth to this, and she is making a good point. It is not that she is unsympathetic and doesn't understand what a person goes through when they have been laid off, but she wants to help the reader move forward. Take this advice as you will. It may resonate with some and rub others the wrong way, but I thought it was worth sharing.

"This sounds harsh. It is intended to sting a bit. At first it sounds like I'm telling you nobody gives a shit about you. The truth is that only a small number of people do, and the rest are either mildly interested or totally indifferent. And none of them, not even those closest to you, are spending a fraction of their waking hours thinking about the fact that you got the boot. Stop acting like you've got something to be embarrassed about because you don't. Any time I network with a colleague in professional transition the first thing I ask them to do is to accept this as their best first step toward

getting themselves out of this purgatory. I care that they are suffering and going through a painful transition. But I don't care that they were fired, and neither will anyone else. The sooner they stop defensively and frantically provide a detailed explanation, the better. I drive this point home by making them hold hands with me over a sticky table in some Starbucks and repeat it after me more than once. I won't let them leave until I've heard these words come out of their mouths: Nobody cares. . . ."[30]

REVISITING BRYANT

I've conducted layoffs firsthand, and I understand what this process looks and feels like. There are two important points for supporting someone going through a layoff. First, it's tough to help the other person feel better about losing their job. Honestly, nothing you say will truly comfort them. It's a difficult situation, and everyone recognizes that. The longer you prolong the conversation, the worse it becomes. Stick to the facts and answer questions briefly. People don't want to discuss this topic after it's happened; it carries feelings of betrayal and shock. I represent the company, which has decided they no longer need you. Very little you say can ease this feeling. So, focus on the essential facts. Understand that the other party isn't seeking a lengthy discussion but still approach it with empathy.

It's not about overdoing it, but about understanding, feeling it, and reading the room during this conversation. Some people may want to get up and walk out, while others prefer to sit and process the information. You have to give people what they want and need at that moment. Empathy is crucial. Since this has happened to most of us, you know how bad it feels. So channel that understanding and recognize what they are experiencing.

Even with my experiences on both sides, when someone tells me they were laid off, I still feel unsure whether to have a career conversation and ask, "What are you looking for?" or if I should engage in an empathetic conversation and ask, "How are you feeling about it?" It depends on what the person wants to discuss; sometimes, they may not want to talk at all. I try to take my cues and guidance from them.

Providing people with language enables them—and you—to discuss a layoff. Here are my suggestions that may help someone navigate the layoff journey. You can ask these questions:

- "How can I help?" (Avoid asking if they're financially strapped, as that can make them feel even worse.)
- "What are you looking for?"
- "Can I connect you with someone?"
- "Would you like to talk about it?"

Offering some questions fosters a safe conversation and can be very helpful. We need to consider how we communicate with those laid off, the questions we ask, and the language we choose, while ensuring we don't make assumptions. Everyone is different and will cope with being laid off in their own way.

WHERE IS BRYANT NOW?

After working with various cannabis startups, Bryant decided to shift his career and broaden his experience by moving to the agency side. In 2021, he became a Managing Director and Partner at a marketing strategy and advertising agency based in Boulder, CO. In his role, he leads the agency's health and wellness initiatives and has secured several notable clients in cannabis and wellness. Recently, he was named CMO, which means that in addition to his client work, he oversees the agency's marketing strategy. Reflecting on his experience, he said, "Every organization has its challenges and flaws—it's just the ones you can manage that keep you motivated. I have loved my time on the agency side—I have learned so much, and I would recommend the leap for anyone looking to truly expand their skill set." Bryant is always open to a chat—you can reach him via his email. b.william.ison@gmail.com.

READER ENGAGEMENT

These reader engagement questions focus on encouraging you to think beyond what you've read in each chapter, continue the conversation, and reflect on your own self-development while also considering how to assist others.

- If someone asks you about your layoff, how do you describe it?
- What do you want people to know about being laid off?
- How can we change the conversation about being laid off?
- How can we remove the shame, guilt, embarrassment, and judgment about being laid off?
- What is your advice to someone who has just been laid off?
- What conversations should we have about layoffs?
- How can companies do better when it comes to layoffs?
- What messaging should companies use during a layoff?

CHAPTER 10

Survivor's Guilt After Layoffs

So you survived a layoff at your company, especially if you've been at a company that is conducting mass layoffs that we all have heard about and know all too well. We continue to read about these layoffs in the headlines and hear about them in the news, and we can't seem to get away from them. We know someone who has either been directly impacted, you've gone through it, or your company continues to struggle, with the chance that it will lead to a layoff. None of these scenarios are ideal and, unfortunately, are inevitable. A significant amount of emotional energy is expended by those who remain at the company after a layoff. The main energy is spent thinking, "Am I next?" or "Why me?" There is so much emotional fatigue associated with survivor's guilt. We know the importance of focusing on those the layoff has directly impacted. Still, we must pay attention and bring awareness to survivor's guilt and the tremendous impact the layoff has on those remaining at the company. As you can see, the collateral damage is felt all around and doesn't go away in an instant; life doesn't go on as usual after such an event of being laid off.

Here is a list of questions you may have asked yourself if you've survived a layoff:

- I survived this one, but will others come, and when will it happen to me?
- Why were those people laid off while I wasn't?
- I can't believe how they laid off my colleagues; it was so insensitive. Will this happen to me?
- If they are downsizing, what will happen to all the work that still needs to be done? Will I be expected to take it on in addition to my own work?
- Are they being honest with us about what is really happening with the company, and what are we not being told?
- Is my job safe or should I start looking for another job?

A study of over 4,000 employees who survived a round of corporate layoffs by Leadership IQ found that: "If your company is undertaking a layoff, be forewarned: Your surviving employees are not going to work harder out of gratitude. This study by Leadership IQ discovered that 74% of employees who kept their job amidst a corporate layoff say their own productivity has declined since the layoff. And 69% say the quality of their company's product or service has declined since the layoffs. We call this Layoff Survivor Stress (a.k.a. Survivor's Guilt). There is a great myth that following a layoff or downsizing, the surviving employees will be so grateful that they still have a job that they'll work harder and be more productive. But as this study shows, the opposite is usually true (and that layoffs place a heavy burden on surviving employees)."[31]

During this time, a significant question that comes into play for the employees left at the company is how much they feel valued by the organization. When downsizing occurs, employees often feel undervalued, resulting in a perceived lack of empathy and transparency. Anger, anxiety, and guilt often characterize those who remain. This atmosphere affects the likelihood of employees staying at the company or recommending it to others. The key takeaway is that leaders and organizations must improve their approach to layoffs. They should prioritize openness, transparency, empathy, and compassion. Above all, they must support everyone and recognize that this situation involves human capital, not human collateral.

After reading this chapter, you will be better equipped to address your needs and to understand the landscape of survivor's guilt following a layoff. As we have learned, it is not just the person directly affected by the layoff but also those employees who remain and the company itself.

You will also be introduced to Jeremy, who graciously shared his story about being laid off, providing a different perspective on survivor's guilt. Jeremy's story is unique; he was laid off but stayed with the company for another year to lead the transition after an acquisition. His experience of survivor's guilt was different, yet it still affected him in profound ways.

INTERVIEW WITH JEREMY: "I WOKE UP WITH A SMILE"

The layoffs were conducted in waves, with many individuals already let go the day before. Despite the snowstorm that day, people felt it was necessary to be in the office. They even contacted employees on vacation to inform them of their termination, not waiting for their return to the office.

It was crazy because I remember people waiting at their desks. No one was doing any work. Everything in the company had come to a halt. People stood by their phones, waiting for the "phone call." You didn't want to leave your desk for anything—not lunch, not even to take a break. We just waited.

At this point, I still wasn't sure if I would lose my job. I had a feeling I would be let go, but it was still uncertain. Then I received the dreaded call. I remember walking into this room. There was a ton of junk, a table, a woman from HR, and the vice president from the new company that had acquired us. At that moment, I was shaking and didn't know what to say because I'd seen some of my friends return from having the "talk." Some people carried the infamous blue folder with the letter because they had been let go, while others walked out without the folder; they were staying. I walked in and sat down, and it felt surreal because I remember the guy looked at me and said, "Unfortunately, we have to eliminate your position."

They try to be nice, but all you want is the blue folder and to move on after receiving this type of news. I knew what was in the folder and what it signified. You get the folder, walk out of the room, feel a bit shaky and try to shake it off, and want to return to your desk. Everyone was eager to know what happened and kept asking questions. That's when it hits you. There was a mix of relief and anxiety because it had been a year and a half in the making.

The company had been enduring such turmoil for so long. There was a sense of relief in knowing there was finally an answer—because for the past year, I had been living with the uncertainty of whether I'd be let go, which puts your life on hold. At least it was over; I finally had my answer. So that day, I got laid off. But I wasn't gone quite yet. They informed me in the spring of 2018 that I had been laid off, but I was allowed to stay until the end of January 2019. I had almost a year to lounge around and assist them in the transition since the senior staff were let go immediately.

The first few weeks after I was laid off felt strange. You have that I don't care, whatever attitude, which was difficult for me to adopt; it's not in my nature. Side note—when my company closed on the merger, which we all knew was happening, I cleaned out my desk months before I was actually laid off. Once the deal was finalized for the acquisition, everyone at the company stopped working. I had gone from working so much to doing nothing. I had nothing else to do, so I just cleaned. In my mind, I knew what was happening. It was coming. So I got ready for it. And then, when they told me, "You have till the end of January," I was like, "Okay. Well, at least my desk is clean!"

I coped by continuing to work because I was deeply invested in this place. Honestly, the business wouldn't have survived if we hadn't helped them. There was some satisfaction in knowing that, and I grew personally during that time. That was what kept me going at the end of the day. I felt like I had put much of my life on hold during this period. We didn't go on vacation and avoided spending too much money because we were so worried about what would happen.

My immediate vice president left shortly after the announcement, so I took on most of her responsibilities. That put me into a more visible role, which I had wanted, and I was thrown into the fire. Suddenly, I became the person assigned to four transition committees. I oversaw a team of twelve, guiding them through the transition. I led meetings with representatives from the new company, coordinated team meetings, relayed information to them, and assisted them in the transition. I felt that my management skills sharpened during that period, accompanied by significant experience in project management. This is where my professional growth began to take off.

I believe it gave me more confidence in my skill sets. I've always felt that you need to promote people before they're ready because you've got to push them out of their comfort zones. That's what it did for me. It forced me out of my comfort zone and gave me confidence because, suddenly, I became the subject matter expert. When you're doing it all the time, you don't realize you are the expert in it. You forget that you know these certain things until you're asked, "What is this? How is this done?" And then I realized, "Wow, I know all of this. I have a wealth of knowledge that these people need to make this work." I definitely think confidence was the thing that helped me the most.

My last day was on a Thursday. So that Friday, I had a big hangover. I woke up late for the first time in a long time and felt a sigh of relief. After so many sleepless nights, I had felt drained. On my first day unemployed, I realized, "It's finally over." I woke up with a smile.

MY RECOVERY

I was mentally exhausted by the end of it. In February, I did nothing but binge-watch TV. I spent a lot of time on the couch, just not ready to think about what came next. I needed to decompress, and honestly, I wouldn't change that because when people go through this kind of thing, it's like a death—an experience where you have to navigate stages. That was my stage of needing to do nothing. I needed to recharge, and that's what I did for the next month.

I truly could not have considered the next step, and I was so thankful for my severance package because I don't think I would have been able to contemplate what to do next without it. I did a lot of walking; it provided me clarity. I know some people went on vacation, some, like me, stayed at home, and others found volunteering helpful. I needed to give myself some time where I didn't think about anything. That's what TV was for me. I remember having this one moment when I thought, oh my God, it's Monday at 11:00 a.m., and I'm not being pulled in twenty-five directions, and I don't have to attend a meeting.

The year leading up to the layoff affected my marriage. We're much stronger now; we got through it, but there were times when it felt like that was all we talked about. It was like the elephant in the room. My husband was only working part-time and was also looking for a job. It became an all-consuming issue for us. Our entire life felt wrapped up in searching for a job and what would happen, and it wore on us. I wouldn't say we drifted apart, but there were sleepless nights for both of us because there was a worry between us: "What's going to happen next?" Knowing I would lose my job anyway, he didn't understand why I worked so hard for these people. We just wanted it to be over and to move on.

YOU SURVIVED A LAYOFF: NOW WHAT?

"Workplace Survivor Syndrome" is a common term used by organizational psychologists in the aftermath of a layoff. This term, coined by organizational psychologists, describes the emotional, psychological, and physical effects on employees who remain in the midst of a company downsizing. Companies must approach these layoffs with compassion, transparency, honesty, and trust for those remaining. We have to look at the impacts on the company from different viewpoints to really understand the entire scope of what we are focusing on.

"Workplace survivor syndrome is a conflation of guilt, betrayal and remorse in employees who've witnessed their colleagues lose their jobs through no fault of their own. Fellow academics have compared the emotional rollercoaster to what people diagnosed with post-traumatic stress disorder (PTSD) experience. Employers must be aware of workplace survivor syndrome and create an emotion processing culture in which employees can identify what they're experiencing," Dr. Silard told HRD. "Whenever people feel trauma, being able to share it helps to mitigate it. If they're not to express their emotions, we'll see them psychosomatize in unhealthy ways, just as we see with loneliness, depression and other challenging emotions."[32]

Of course, the layoff is hard for those it is happening to, but being one of the employees left behind can also be tough. "Layoffs can disrupt a company's culture, lower team morale, and rupture any semblance of psychological safety for the workers to remain. What if that person is you? How do you navigate a rattled workplace looming with uncertainty?"[33]

You will experience intense emotions while remaining at a company after a layoff. It is okay to be honest with yourself about feeling relieved that you still have your job. These feelings are very real; you shouldn't feel guilty about them. You should honor your emotions, acknowledge them, and understand how they might keep you stuck where you are or help you move forward. There will be emotional, mental, and physical impacts during a time like a layoff or a traumatic event such as this. What do you do with all of this? How do you navigate through this process to take care of yourself, your loved ones, and your co-workers? If you are struggling to take care of yourself, let alone anyone else, it will be difficult.

What makes sense for your well-being and career trajectory? Do you know how to take care of yourself during this time? Below are some practical suggestions for you to consider. However, please remember that you need to determine the version that works best for you.

1. **Acknowledge and accept your feelings about the situation:**
    a. You've survived the layoff and will experience a flood of emotions. You may feel relief that you still have a job, along with anger, guilt, anxiety, and fear, to name a few.
    b. Take a moment to sit with these feelings, absorb them, and acknowledge them, then determine how to move forward.
    c. Lean on your co-workers, loved ones, a mental health professional, or anyone who can help you navigate through these emotions.

2. **Remember your "Why" and your value:**
    a. Everything comes into question during a layoff, whether you are directly impacted by it or have survived the layoff at your company. So, remember why you do the work you do, why you chose to work at that company, and most importantly, remember what gives you purpose and meaning.
    b. It is okay to feel sad about what has happened but also remember the value you bring and your worth.

3. **Take time to connect with others and continue building relationships.**
    a. Especially during a period like a layoff, it's important to be around those you trust, who can

provide comfort, who you can support, and who can help you make sense of what is happening.

b. Not only should you stay connected with your current co-workers but also remember to reach out to those who have been laid off. They particularly need these connections; you would hope for the same if you were in their situation. Connection is significant; no matter how big or small, it remains powerful and incredibly important for everyone.

4. **Focus on what you can control:**

a. This involves concentrating on your work, your relationships with co-workers and your boss, your friends, your loved ones, your growth opportunities, and your next step.

b. It also includes managing your stress, burnout, and both your mental and physical health.

5. **Set boundaries for yourself:**

a. After the layoff occurs, there is considerable uncertainty regarding what will happen to you, the work, and the company. Consider what your needs are and what is in your best interest. Value your time.

b. Once the layoff takes place, there is an expectation that business continues as usual, the work must go on, and anyone remaining will be expected to handle that workload. It is not your fault that the layoffs happened; that responsibility lies with the company, so they need to resolve this issue.

c. Determine what is realistic for you in terms of your workload and additional projects you can manage.

d. What is a healthy way to address your stress, burnout, the disrupted work environment, and culture?

6. **Consider seeking help, support, and resources:**

a. Reflect on what you require to navigate this period.

b. Remember to ask for assistance, support, and anything else you need to help you through this transition.

7. **It might be difficult at first, but look for the silver lining:**

a. A layoff can be an important time to reflect on your relationship with your job. It may be an opportunity to pause for a moment and consider where you are and what you truly want with greater intentionality.

b. Contemplate what opportunities may arise during this time. The layoff at the company doesn't have to be a setback for you; instead, it can serve as a chance to re-prioritize your well-being and yourself.

IMPACT OF LAYOFFS ON THE SURVIVOR

An article written by Dr. Beth Kaplan, in which she shared stories of people she knew who had been laid off and were recounting their experiences to her, wrote about Avery, who survived a layoff at her company. Avery's story perfectly sums up the effect that layoffs can have on survivors. "She survived multiple rounds of layoffs, and her company has made her feel as if that's a gift, that she is lucky to have a job. Avery was told to stop focusing on the huge amount of work she now can't split with colleagues or the sadness she feels now that her teammates are gone. After each round, the company hosts what they call "survivor week"—as a thank-you for those left behind. Avery doesn't need a company happy hour; she needs support and resources, including counseling to talk out her feelings. She needs her manager to help her load balance. She needs to know why the layoffs happened and what the company is doing to prevent this from recurring. All of which can help employees feel valued and supported, reducing the impact of survivor's guilt and helping to promote recovery and resilience."[34]

IMPACT OF LAYOFFS ON THE COMPANY

We know that layoffs impact those directly affected and those who remain at the company, and there is a significant effect on the company itself. You may be wondering why you should care. It's understandable that you wouldn't care much about the impact on the company that just laid you off. But this is information that is still valuable and may influence future employment or other decisions. I think it is helpful to understand the full scope of the situation.

The hope is that layoffs will be the last resort for a company and that the aftermath will not be too devastating and traumatic. There will be both short- and long-term effects following a layoff. Companies must prioritize caring for their employees, those who survived the layoffs, and this should be fundamental to how the company moves forward.

Employees will feel angry, upset, anxious, and guilty when such an event occurs. They may hold a grudge, and everything about the company, leadership, and anyone involved in the layoff decision will come into question, especially how the layoff was handled and what happened immediately afterward. Employees will feel frustrated about taking on additional responsibilities, particularly if there are no intentions to replace those who were let go. The company needs to be pragmatic about what can and must be done regarding the expected work. There should not be an automatic assumption that employees will handle more tasks with considerably less support.

Productivity among remaining employees will likely decline significantly after the layoff. This is part of the process and should be incorporated into managing expectations. Morale will likely be low, and many employees will seek other opportunities after a layoff that offer greater security, transparency, trust, and realistic expectations for work, productivity, growth, and cultural changes. Why would an employee want to stay if they can't trust a company?

The company could also take a significant hit to its reputation in the world and with potential employees. A poorly-executed layoff could mean difficulty in hiring top talent in the future. That can lead to increased expenses as it takes longer and costs more to conduct the hiring process, and top talent will likely demand higher pay to compensate for the lack of trust in the company and in anticipation of future potential layoffs.

These are the types of issues companies should take into account when planning a layoff, and they are the also the issues that employees should watch out for when applying for new jobs. If you know you are interviewing for a job with a company that recently had a layoff, ask about it. Ask about their process, the morale, and the other issues outlined above. And if you land a role in management, remember your experience, and encourage the company to adopt more human-centric policies. You may have the power to create this change in the corporate world!

REVISITING JEREMY

As you read at the beginning of the chapter, Jeremy had quite the journey. It was a mental and physical rollercoaster. Let's read about the rest of Jeremy's journey.

ADVICE TO OTHERS

As a financial expert, I suggest that you should have six to twelve months' worth of savings if possible. I understand this isn't feasible for everyone. Before this situation arose, we were saving for an apartment and had our down payment fund, which was not intended to be our emergency money. After this experience, we've both agreed that this should now serve as our emergency fund, and we'll begin saving again for our down payment afterward. This approach allows you the flexibility to decline any job offer and provides peace of mind knowing you won't be homeless in a month. That has been truly beneficial.

We became more fiscally responsible when we

realized this was happening with the company. Before I was officially laid off, I contacted the cable company, the phone company, and the *New York Times*. They all offered me a deal. I managed to reduce our bills by $250 a month. We also started shopping at the grocery store and eating at home more often, and we cut back on going out.

MOVING FORWARD

I've given this a lot of thought; I want to do more to give back in some way. You read stories about people who can't or didn't save, and it can be even more devastating for them, pushing them into poverty or debt. There must be a better way to help others.

I want to be more engaged in all aspects of my life so that I'm fully present, and it's not all about work. I want to get involved in other activities. I can choose how I want this experience to change me or keep me as I am. I want to carve a new path for myself and enjoy my life more. My identity and what I do won't be tied up in my job. There is so much more that I want to do and be. I know what it feels like to be laid off, and who's to say it won't happen again? But if it does, at least I know how to handle it. I will be a better advocate for myself, and I know I will get through it without having to do it alone.

WHERE IS JEREMY NOW?

Jeremy received a job offer about six months after being laid off. It was a better position as VP of Finance for a large media company. He has been there ever since, leading a team of twelve. During his time off, he applied to graduate school and earned his MBA in August 2022. Jeremy and his husband moved out of the city and purchased a house in the suburbs. Ultimately, he is very glad he was let go from his old company, is no longer in publishing, and is now working for a digital-forward firm.

READER ENGAGEMENT

You can never be fully prepared for a layoff, whether it affects you directly or if you survive one at your company. As we have learned, layoffs are handled in ways some of us never imagined, and companies do not often approach them with compassion. However, some companies manage this better than others, and we need to recognize and acknowledge those.

We hope that layoffs will be a last resort, but it doesn't always turn out that way. So how can we best prepare for and deal with something so traumatic when it occurs, and move forward in a healthy and constructive manner? One that will set you up for success both now and in the future. The questions below are designed to help you reflect on your current situation and what lies ahead.

- How can you establish boundaries with your current work and any work that may be expected of you after a layoff?
- What type of conversation can you have with your boss or manager to ensure clear expectations?
- What steps would you like to take to protect yourself from another possible round of layoffs at your company?
- Were the laid off employees treated with dignity, respect, sensitivity, and concern?
- Did management give a meaningful explanation for

the downsizing? Were they open with you about what was happening?

- What does it look like if you remain in your job after a layoff?
- Are you ready to consider a job search if layoffs occur at your company?

CHAPTER 11

Mental Health In the Workplace and Beyond

Is there a mental health practice or wellness program at your workplace? Is mental health a topic of conversation within your company? Do you feel at ease discussing your own mental health challenges at work or with your boss? Are you aware of the resources available to support your well-being and wellness in the workplace?

These are important questions to consider and discuss with your employer. Mental health in the workplace is a critical issue that should be prioritized by both individuals and organizations. How many headlines have you seen lately about rising burn-out rates, increasing stress levels, and the growing number of employees leaving their jobs due to toxic workplace cultures or a lack of mental health support? This topic is not going away and should remain a priority every day.

According to Forbes, here is a quick snapshot of what mental health and well-being currently look like in the workplace:

- 92% of workers say it is very (57%) or somewhat (35%) important to them to work for an organization that values their emotional and psychological well-being.

- 92% believe it is very (52%) or somewhat (40%) important to them to work for an organization that provides support for employee mental health.
- 95% report that it is very (66%) or somewhat (29%) important to them to feel respected at work.
- 95% feel it is very (61%) or somewhat (34%) important to them to work for an organization that respects the boundaries between work and nonwork time.
- 67% of workers feel they work in a toxic environment (up 4% from 2023).
- 78% of workers don't think their employer is doing enough to address their mental wellness at work (up 3% from 2023).
- 61% of workers would rather quit, and 39% would rather get laid off from their job than work in a toxic workplace.[35]

This should encourage us to explore this topic further and use this information effectively to create a path toward enhancing our mental health and well-being.

In this chapter, you will read about a young woman's journey with her mental health at work and how it has impacted her life. We will discuss mental health in the workplace, its effects on individuals, and what true mental health and well-being should look like in work environments. Finally, we will explore how to turn awareness into action and what this means for all of us.

In the following interview, you will meet Ellie, who bravely shared her story about her mental health challenges, particularly in the workplace. Anyone facing their own mental health concerns or knowing someone who is struggling should find connections to Ellie and comfort in realizing they are not alone. What impressed me most about Ellie was her openness and honesty regarding her mental health. Her narrative effectively illustrates why mental health in the workplace requires greater attention from corporate leaders for their employees.

Ellie advocated for herself during a critical time in her life. Many readers of her interview may view her decision to take mental health leave as a risk. However, this should not be deemed a risk but rather a necessity—something that should become standard in the workplace when someone is struggling and needs to prioritize their mental health.

Think about how many people you know who would actually take a break from work to focus on their mental health and well-being. The answer is likely not many. Instead, most individuals remain in their current situations, failing to advocate for themselves or express their needs, especially in the workplace. This is quite common, and it's important to remember that there isn't a right or wrong way to handle such situations; you should do what works for you and use what is accessible to you.

The good news is that more people are beginning to explore the option of taking mental health breaks and realizing that prioritizing their well-being is a worthwhile investment.

One in five Americans suffer from some sort of mental health condition, but more than half don't receive treatment.[36] Think about it this way: if you are sitting in a room with your closest friends, at least one of them is suffering, so this is an important statistic to acknowledge. Furthermore, it indicates that these conditions impact one's physical health, job performance, and employee productivity. Prioritizing mental health in the workplace should be a standard ethical responsibility that employers uphold for their employees.

INTERVIEW WITH ELLIE: "WE NEED A VOICE AND A PLATFORM"

I was let go on the morning of August 1, 2019. It was my first day back after three months of medical leave, and I was quite shocked, even though I almost expected it. That day, I had a feeling I can't quite explain—it was just one of those gut feelings you get every so often right before something bad is about to happen. A few people on my team had already been let go, and a subconscious feeling suggested that something was off. Everything was too quiet.

The day I returned to work, I received texts from friends and family, "Have a great first day back. You're doing the right thing." Everybody knew that I wasn't really ready to go back. They knew I was returning for financial reasons and needed to get back to a routine. I was hoping it would feel different this time.

On my first day back, I worked remotely. I logged onto my computer and checked a few emails, but I didn't end up responding to any of them because I was nervous about the conference call with my boss. I was mainly anxious about talking to her for the first time in three months, and I wasn't sure how the call would go. The conversation was, "How are things going?" and then I was let go.

The reason I was let go was due to "restructuring." I was part of the corporate marketing and communications team, and they were reorganizing the group.

While I haven't personally fired anyone, I've participated in management teams during layoffs, and repeatedly, the rationale for letting someone go is, "We're letting him go because of restructuring." It's the ultimate ambiguous term that denies any sense of closure.

I took a leave for mental health reasons. This decision was something I never expected to make, despite my lifelong struggles with mental health. While on vacation, I worked, which eventually led to a breakdown. When I discussed this with my psychiatrist, she described it as a severe anxiety attack, along with a situational episode. It incapacitated me from going to work, an outcome I never intended. I am now focused on ensuring this does not happen again and recognizing the warning signs earlier.

I worked nights and weekends, going above and beyond what was expected of me because I believed there was a carrot at the end of the stick—an opportunity I was pursuing. Ironically, I felt relief when I was let go because it wasn't the right culture for me. After the layoff, it's strange how you can go from feeling like a company woman, part of the inner circle, to suddenly feeling alone. I was alone and needed to advocate for myself in a way I had never done before.

I felt immediate anger when it happened. I quickly became stressed about figuring out what to do next. The "in the moment" life questions took over: "What are my options for negotiating severance? What do I have to do about unemployment? How do I return my computer to the company?" All these questions and thoughts were swirling around. Getting to what mattered was difficult: "What do I want to do with the rest of my life? How will I maintain some of the wonderful connections and experiences from that job, including people who will, hopefully, be lifelong connections?"

The day after I was laid off, I went full throttle—focused on getting things done. That's generally how I handle things. Over the next two months, I accomplished a lot. I took two trips, visiting my parents in Cincinnati and going to California to see my boyfriend. I did some heavy networking and had meetings with the women in my B2B marketing group; they were fantastic, and it was exactly what I needed, even though I didn't always feel up to it. Anything that involves putting on pants doesn't sound fun when you're unemployed, but I forced myself to get out there. I worked on finishing tasks that had piled up; I was filling my days with "stuff." You must be careful because the minute you clear the queue, more stuff keeps flooding through the cracks that need to be done. I reorganized my apartment a lot. I took long walks, and I remember that it took longer to do things than necessary because I had the time. For example, walking to therapy and returning home took half a day when it would usually be a lunch break.

I was already seeing a therapist and a psychiatrist when I was laid off. I had an appointment with my psychiatrist the week after I was let go, and when I told her what had happened, she was shocked and impressed by how I handled everything. I was sad and crying, and she said, "The you I met a few months ago would not have been okay. You are so much more stable." That felt great to hear.

I've experienced anxiety and depression my whole life, but my psychiatrist realized I was likely more bipolar, which is often misdiagnosed. She treated me with medication, and therapy was also helping. Overall, the treatment helped me cope with being laid off, but I needed constant reminders from my doctors to say, "You seem like you're handling this well." She helped me understand that my feelings matter and that I should tell her when I feel depressed. Even if I feel bad, she sees someone who is getting things done, getting up, and accomplishing something every day.

MENTAL HEALTH IN THE WORKPLACE

Every year, the month of May is dedicated to National Mental Health Awareness, which is a good start, but we really need to be attentive to mental health needs all year long. Ellie's words and genuine emotions while sharing her experiences provided insight into how the workplace affected her mental health, how her company failed to support her, and why businesses need to improve in this area.

"ComPsych, the largest provider of employee mental health and absence management services, released new data that shows mental health related leaves of absence continue to skyrocket among U.S. workers. From 2017 to 2023, mental health leaves of absence have increased by 300%. In 2023 alone, mental health related leaves of absence increased by 33% over the prior year. In 2023, women took nearly seven in ten (69%) of all mental health related leaves of absence. Millennial women accounted for one-third (33%) of 2023 mental health related leaves of absence, followed by Gen X women, who accounted for 30%."[37]

Hearing Elie's story deepened my understanding of her experiences and underscored the importance of compassion and kindness. It reinforced the necessity of discussing mental health not only in the workplace but in all aspects of life. Additionally, it emphasized the significance of creating long-term plans and taking actionable steps to support those in need. I am now more aware of how I can better assist my clients who may be facing similar challenges.

It's important to start with the definition of mental health. The World Health Organization (WHO) definition states, "Mental health is a state of mental well-being that enables people to cope with the stresses of life, realize their abilities, learn well and work well, and contribute to their community. It is an integral component of health and well-being that underpins our individual and collective abilities to make decisions, build relationships, and shape the world we live in. Mental health is a basic human right. And it is crucial to personal, community and socio-economic development."[38]

Now that we know the definition of mental health, let's define it in the workplace. In my research, I came across a website, Hibob.com, an HR platform, that states, "Mental health in the workplace refers to employees' psychological, emotional, and social well-being within a shared work environment."[39]

There has been a significant shift among employees and employers regarding mental health needs in recent years. Mental health concerns and mental health in the workplace have always existed. The change is that people are now discussing it more openly. There is heightened awareness, reduced stigma, and increased efforts to support those facing mental health challenges and to cultivate an environment that prioritizes mental health. Companies are beginning to reassess their mental health infrastructure, although much work remains to be done. We are witnessing professional athletes, politicians, and celebrities integrating mental health into their brands and fostering safe spaces to discuss their own mental health experiences. They are making the topic less taboo and more a part of mainstream conversations. Just as we invest in our physical health, we need to invest in our mental health and treat ourselves as whole individuals. We need to establish self-awareness and prioritize mental health as a new healthy habit in our regular lifestyle practices.

New research from Deloitte shows that "The vast majority of the C-suite (77%) believes workforce mental health well-being improved last year, but only 33% of employees agree. In fact, 25% of employees say their mental health *got worse,* and about half of employees say they feel stressed or exhausted "often" or "always." Just 3 percent of the C-suit recognize this in their workforce."[40] To bring this to light, "Sixty percent of employees are considering quitting their jobs to work for an employer that takes better care of their mental well-being. That's a big risk for employers struggling to attract talent."[41]

An important note before we proceed: do not self-diagnose or make assumptions about your mental health. Instead, consult a mental health professional and work with those who can accurately diagnose, treat, and support you.

It's important to recognize and understand the most prevalent mental health issues in the workplace and how to address them, even if you are not a mental health professional. Based on my research, and in my experience with my clients, the most common mental health issues in the workplace are *anxiety, depression, stress, and substance abuse or misuse.*

Do you truly understand what anxiety, depression, stress, and substance abuse or misuse involve? These concepts may seem simple, but having clear definitions for each can shed light on your feelings and encourage you to delve deeper into your own mental health, if you haven't already done so. The American Psychological Association provides the following definitions for us:

1. **Anxiety:** "Anxiety is an emotion characterized by feelings of tension, worried thoughts, and physical changes like increased blood pressure. People

with anxiety disorders usually have recurring intrusive thoughts or concerns. They may avoid certain situations out of worry. They may also have physical symptoms such as sweating, trembling, dizziness, or a rapid heartbeat."

2. **Depression:** "Depression is extreme sadness or despair that lasts more than days. It interferes with the activities of daily life and can cause physical symptoms such as pain, weight loss or gain, sleeping pattern disruptions, or lack of energy. People with depression may also experience an inability to concentrate, feelings of worthlessness or excessive guilt, and recurrent thoughts of death or suicide."

3. **Stress:** "Stress is a normal reaction to everyday pressures but can become unhealthy when it upsets your day-to-day functioning. Stress involves changes affecting nearly every system of the body, influencing how people feel and behave. By causing mind-body changes, stress contributes directly to psychological and physiological disorder and disease and affects mental and physical health, reducing the quality of life."

4. **Substance Abuse:** "Substance abuse is a pattern of compulsive substance use marked by recurrent significant social, occupational, legal, or interpersonal adverse consequences, such as repeated absences from work or school, arrests, and marital difficulties. Addiction is a state of

psychological or physical dependence (or both) on the use of alcohol or other drugs. The term is often used as an equivalent term for substance dependence and sometimes applied to behavioral disorders, such as sexual, internet, and gambling addictions."[42]

The Center for Workplace Mental Health, a division of the American Psychiatric Association Foundation, emphasizes the importance of recognizing the warning signs of depression and anxiety. The center states, "The more we know about the warning signs of common conditions in the workplace, like depression and anxiety, the more proactive we can be in supporting ourselves and others."[43]

Depression warning signs include:
- Trouble sleeping or sleeping too much
- Feeling sad
- Loss of interest in activities previously enjoyed and social withdrawal
- Difficulty concentrating and making decisions
- Changes in appetite, overeating, or not eating enough
- Fatigue
- Restless activity or slowed movements and speech
- Feelings of worthlessness or guilt
- Thoughts of suicide or self-harm

Anxiety warning signs include:
- Excessive worry
- Feeling nervous, irritable, or on edge

- Sense of impending danger, panic, or doom
- Increased heart rate
- Breathing rapidly (hyperventilation), sweating, and/ or trembling
- Feeling weak or tired
- Difficulty concentrating
- Trouble sleeping
- Gastrointestinal (GI) problems

Here is a simple checklist and mental health self-check-in questions to help you manage your mental health.

Checklist items	Date to Complete	Date Completed	Notes
Take an inventory of your mental health			
Learn about the warning signs of depression, anxiety, substance use, abuse, and burnout			
Ask for help			
Create your support system to help you manage your mental health			

Checklist items	Date to Complete	Date Completed	Notes
Make sure you are taking care of the following: - Making sleep a priority - Eating healthy - Getting enough exercise - Setting goals - Setting boundaries - Making time for things you enjoy - Staying connected with family and friends - Taking time to relax			
Identify tools and resources to help you (Apps, talking to someone, self-help books, wellness programs, etc.)			
Consistently check in with people			
Add anything else you feel would be necessary on the checklist.			

20 MENTAL HEALTH SELF-CHECK-IN QUESTIONS

1. How do I feel about life and the work I'm doing right now?

2. Am I feeling stressed? What are the causes of my stress?

3. How am I coping with challenges and stressors?

4. What kind of reoccurring thoughts are negatively impacting me?

5. Am I feeling exhausted more often than before? Is this happening sporadically or am I always exhausted?

6. How am I responding to challenging situations?

7. Have I been more irritable or easily angered about situations that in the past wouldn't have made me feel this way?

8. Do I feel valued by my peers and leaders at work? Do I feel valued by myself?

9. Can I concentrate on the tasks at hand? Or am I getting more easily distracted and off-track when working on something?

10. Do I have personal boundaries that both others and I respect? Do I have any personal boundaries at all? How am I "enforcing" these personal boundaries?

11. How is my sleep doing these days? Am I sleeping enough? Am I getting quality sleep?

12. Am I properly regulating my emotions or unconsciously snapping at people?

13. Am I finding enjoyment in the activities I do in life and work?

14. Am I feeling motivated?

15. How am I connecting with others? How am I maintaining healthy relationships with coworkers

and my loved ones? How am I managing conflicts
with those around me?

16. What am I noticing about my mental health and
overall well-being that worries me?

17. How is my energy level?

18. Are there things that are activating positive
emotions in me? What kinds of things?

19. Am I spending time on self-care? What activities
am I participating in to enhance my mental health
and overall well-being?

20. Do I need help? Can I recognize situations that I
can't manage on my own and that require support
from others, including professional health care?

WHAT MENTAL HEALTH IN THE WORKPLACE SHOULD LOOK LIKE

We are seeing that an increasing number of employees expect
their employers to provide mental health support. Lyra Health
conducted a State of Workplace Mental Survey of 1,000 plus
workers. They found that "84% said "Robust and comprehensive" mental health benefits were an important factor when
considering a new job." In addition, "81% of employee benefits
leaders surveyed believe it is an employer's responsibility to
prevent work-related mental health problems from developing
among employees."[44] So what is this telling us? This survey
illustrates that:

1. Companies must create a culture of mental health
well-being, awareness, and psychological safety.

2. Employees want and need mental health support in the workplace.

3. There are significant benefits of incorporating awareness and support in the workplace.

4. There are plenty of tools and resources that should be available in the workplace to address mental health.

5. People want to know that they can talk about their mental health and feel supported and safe to communicate their needs.

Employees are expressing a growing need for more flexibility in work schedules, mental health days, and extended company closures to promote mental health breaks. They advocate for a culture of work-life balance, which includes setting boundaries for email expectations after hours and on weekends, as well as encouraging regular breaks throughout the day. Furthermore, there is a strong desire for a culture in which leaders and managers can recognize the signs of burnout. Most importantly, the culture must normalize and encourage conversations about mental health. As you review this list of employee needs, I encourage you to reflect on what is important to you and what you need to feel supported. While we focus on mental health in the workplace, consider what you require from your company, yourself, and your overall well-being.

What does mental health support look like for companies? Ideally, more employers will invest in workplace mental health solutions and improve access to quality tools, resources, and comprehensive programs. This should provide insight into what can be achieved in a company to support employees' mental health.

Here is a great example of how one particular company ensures a comprehensive approach to improving mental health awareness and action in the workplace. "General Dynamics Information Technology, a global enterprise with 30,000 employees, launched its "How Are You Really?" campaign in 2021 after an employee died by suicide. The campaign raises awareness around mental health and fosters discussions about what supports, in terms of interventions, benefits, flexibility and culture change, GDIT's people need from each other and from the company." The President of GDIT, Amy Gilliland, said, "This includes reprioritizing workloads, allowing people to take meaningful paid time off to rebalance, and flexing people's hours. We've received an overwhelming response to 'How Are You Really?' Almost every day, an employee tells me about how the campaign has helped them."[45]

SHIFTING AWARENESS TO ACTION

There is a consensus that companies must do better to support their employees' mental health. You've read Ellie's story about what happened to her when her company lacked mental health support, you've seen the statistics illustrating the mental health crisis, you've observed the impact on companies when action is not taken, and you've also read about a company that is effectively supporting their employees.

Now, let's focus on what to look for in your current company and potential future employers, as well as how this might look in practice. Companies can take numerous steps to foster a culture of mental health awareness and proactive support. We'll begin with the most fundamental first step: recognizing the need for mental health support and committing to addressing it for both the company and its employees. After conducting extensive research for this chapter and engaging with various individuals, here's a list of what to consider in your current workplace or when job hunting.

- A culture of awareness, support, and a safe space where discussions about mental health are encouraged, rather than judged, looked down upon, or held against the person. An environment where individuals feel comfortable talking about their mental health and asking for help if needed.
- Training for managers, HR professionals, and company leaders to address mental health and fundamental health practices.
- Mental health support, tools, resources, and benefits: Here are some suggested resources that should be available to employees: Inquire about what is available to you if it has not already been communicated.
    - › EAP (Employee Assistance Program): This should be available to all employees. If you're unsure whether your company offers it, please inquire. If you are searching for a job, this is an excellent question to ask during the interview to understand the mental health support the company provides.
    - › Subscriptions to online apps: Many excellent apps are available to provide support. If your company doesn't offer this, ask if they can cover

the cost or suggest making it available for their employees.

› Health insurance that provides mental health coverage and services.

› Access to wellness programs: If your company doesn't provide them, identify one that you would like to participate in. Inquire if your company will invest in it for the employees. If not, see if they will cover the cost or reimburse you for it.

› Other resources and tools that can support you include self-help books, podcasts, and information shared across the company, such as articles.

• Workers should feel supported and not guilty for taking necessary time off. Companies must recognize that mental health is a challenge, not a weakness.

While writing this chapter, I learned that when all the conditions are in place to undertake meaningful mental health care, when there is strength and program conviction, and when action is taken, significant, meaningful change and impact can occur. If companies invest in their employees, they will reap the best from them; just as when you invest in yourself, everyone gets the best of you. It's a win-win for everyone.

REVISITING ELLIE

One thing that has come from this entire experience is that I've never been so open about my mental illness before, despite having dealt with it my whole life. I have drawn on strengths I didn't realize I had. By becoming more aware of myself, I'm getting up every day and doing something, whether it's big or small; I continue to work on myself, which is significant, but I'm also focusing on the external aspect, meaning what comes next. There's no hesitation in my voice when I talk about mental illness. I own it; it's part of who I am, and I need to embrace it. I am giving it a voice and a platform.

We need to discuss mental health in the workplace. I don't think companies fully support having these conversations. We are beginning to understand it, but we haven't fully embraced it. We need to change this and start talking about it and acknowledging it. The challenging part is that the real problem is deeply rooted in our culture. I know part of what I have is hereditary, but culturally, it's difficult even to differentiate. I believe more open and honest discussions about mental illness need to take place. The forced conversations we've had about sexual harassment and similar issues need to happen with mental illness, too.

I know companies are struggling to address mental health issues and burnout. I understand it isn't easy, but we must find balance. Workplaces need to initiate conversations and acknowledge these challenges. Regular webinars, training, and discussions about burnout must also take place. Sensitivity around this subject is essential; it needs to be addressed, but the approach to the discussion matters. If someone cannot afford therapy, there are alternative solutions. Many companies offer an Employee Assistance Program (EAP), enabling employees to seek the support they need. When someone goes through onboarding at a company, is this information shared, or is it overlooked? What steps are companies taking to engage employees regarding mental health and burnout?

Companies should have mental health program information available every day. It can be as simple as posting an article about mental illness within the company or sharing a daily thought, such as, "Do you know someone who is struggling? What should you do if you see someone in need? Are you struggling? What options do you have?" Don't get me wrong; some companies excel at recognizing it and weaving it into their culture. However, there is still much more work to be done.

I firmly believe there should be a dedicated position in every company to promote mental health, similar to the DEI role found in many businesses. Even a company like the one I recently left recognized that its employees were experiencing burnout. While it may not be possible to completely resolve the issue, it's important to acknowledge what's happening. At the very least, managers should receive training to identify burnout in their teams and themselves. Often, a manager—I've been guilty of this—will become burned out and inadvertently worsen the situation for everyone, as it tends to trickle down.

HOW DO WE TALK ABOUT BEING LAID OFF AND MENTAL HEALTH?

Talking about being laid off is a difficult subject for many people. It's seldom part of our everyday conversations. This creates a dilemma: How can we address this issue when discussions about both layoffs and mental health are often missing? It's surprising, given the numerous platforms available for these conversations. There are spaces specifically designed for discussing mental health, such as texting or online forums. I was especially encouraged by a Talkspace commercial featuring Olympic gold medal swimmer Michael Phelps where he stresses the importance of seeking help.

We aren't discussing mental health enough, nor are we adequately addressing job loss. I'm surprised by how many people haven't asked me about it, especially given my situation. People often don't know what to say, but I wish they would still reach out and not be afraid to talk about it with me. There are two sides to this issue. How can we create a space where those of us who have been laid off can share our experiences with more confidence and lead conversations about it? Additionally, friends, family, and former colleagues should feel comfortable speaking with someone who has faced a layoff. Whatever the reason, it's important for others to engage in these discussions and connect with someone going through this experience. I intend to talk openly about my layoff for the rest of my career. If I want to support others, I need to integrate this experience into my story, both professionally and personally.

WHAT IS YOUR MESSAGE TO ANYONE READING THIS?

You need to rely on yourself to take care of your mental health in order to navigate these situations and advocate for yourself. Everyone has the ability to change their circumstances, and I only wish I had taken action sooner before someone else made decisions for me. If anything, being laid off was both a relief and a wake-up call. It made me realize that we must prioritize our well-being at work, whether it's before or after something happens. Regardless of our employment status, the most crucial thing is to care for ourselves; our physical and mental health are integral to that. We can't always control the decisions made about our well-being, nor can we dictate how quickly companies respond to these issues. However, we can raise our voices, engage in conversations, and do whatever we can, even if it's something small, to support those who are struggling and ourselves.

WHERE IS ELLIE NOW?

Ellie moved to Cincinnati and resumed her career leading content marketing for a tech startup. The job loss and subsequent mental health wake-up call helped her realize that she wanted to be closer to family and focus on what matters. She shares that it remains a daily struggle to maintain her mental health in the fast-paced world of marketing, but being in a welcoming environment that embraces nontraditional thinking and supports mental health makes a difference.

READER ENGAGEMENT

These questions will hopefully assist you in developing your own awareness of mental health and understanding how to ensure you are taking care of yourself and feeling supported in all aspects of your life. If you haven't done so, please familiarize yourself with the tools and resources available to you at your current workplace.

- Are you struggling with mental health issues, and do you know your options or how to seek help?
- Do you know somebody struggling with mental health, and what to do if you see somebody struggling?
- Have you taken an inventory of your mental health? Do you know how to do this?
- Do you know the signs or symptoms of mental health issues? Especially anxiety, depression, stress, substance abuse, and burnout.
- Can you recognize when your mental health is affecting your body (physical self)?

- How do your body and mind respond to stress and burnout?
- What kind of mental health support do you need in the workplace?
- How did your current or previous company engage you in a conversation about mental health and burnout?
- What mental health tools and resources are available to you in your workplace?
- How would you ask your manager/boss or HR for support regarding burnout and your mental health?

ADDITIONAL RESOURCES

- National Alliance on Mental Health: www.nami.org
- National Institute on Mental Health: https://www.nimh.nih.gov
- 988: Suicide and Crisis Lifeline- 988lifeline.org
- OpenMD: openmd.com/directory/psych
- American Psychiatric Association. Accessed at https://www.psychiatry.org/patients-families/depression/what-is-depression
- American Psychiatric Association. Accessed at https://www.psychiatry.org/patients-families/anxiety-disorders/what-are-anxiety-disorders
- World Health Organization: Guidelines on Mental Health At Work: https://www.who.int/publications/i/item/9789240053052
- Center for Disease and Prevention: https://www.cdc.gov/workplacehealthpromotion/tools-resources/workplace-health/mental-health/index.html

CHAPTER 12

It Was the Best Gift, Just in the
Ugliest Wrapping Paper

I can hardly believe that I am sitting here writing the second part of my story and having the opportunity to share my journey with you. A lot has happened since I left my job in 2013. I am amazed that something as devastating and disruptive as being laid off could impact me in such a profound way—ways I never imagined—and turn my life into something extraordinary.

I went through a significant period of self-reflection and discovery, and I realized that it is valuable to periodically assess your life. This involves looking at where you are, how you got there, what you've accomplished, and where you want to go. It's also important to examine the challenges you've faced and the situations in your life that may not have turned out as expected, recognizing that everything happens for a reason. Consider what you've learned from these experiences.

We often don't take the time to pause, breathe, and reflect enough. We tend to keep rushing through the hectic pace of our lives. However, what we have done up to this point is just as important and can serve as a valuable tool for our future growth.

Why wait for a significant event to inspire reflection? Instead, consider making it a regular practice in your life. I can assure you that you will be grateful for it. I truly believe that everything in our lives happens for a reason. People enter our lives for a purpose, regardless of how long they stay; even a brief encounter can have a profound impact. Every decision we make and every choice we face has a reason behind it. We may not understand the reasons at the time, but everything happens for a purpose.

After being laid off, I planned to find another job in the substance abuse field, and my career search was leading me in that direction—until one day, everything changed. To be completely transparent, becoming a coach wasn't a path I had considered. It happened by chance. The career coach I was working with asked me the most powerful question anyone had ever posed to me: "Have you ever thought about becoming a coach?" I looked at her with confusion, thinking, "What is this coaching thing you speak of?" I hadn't heard much about coaching, and when I did, it was only in passing.

In retrospect, this was the defining moment that changed everything for me. Something clicked, and everything became incredibly clear. I honestly wish I could explain what happened, but all I know is that it simply did. I felt as though a weight had been lifted off my shoulders regarding the next step in my career. It was something far outside my comfort zone because I didn't know enough about it. However, that didn't stop me from learning everything I could about coaching: exploring different coaching programs, talking to other coaches, and studying the coaching industry to understand its direction and how I could fit into this world. The more information I gathered, the clearer coaching became as my next career move.

The day I got laid off unexpectedly became the best thing that ever happened to me. It was truly "the best gift in the ugliest wrapping paper." I had always been the kind of person who sat on the edge of the pool, dipping a toe in the water but never taking the plunge, making a splash, or diving into the deep end. Losing my job was exactly what I needed to take that next step.

As I delved into my exploration and research, I discovered that becoming a coach was the right path for me. With nearly twenty years of experience in the substance abuse field and a therapeutic background, I have always enjoyed helping others. In fact, I had engaged in coaching at various points throughout my career. Given this experience, it felt like a natural choice to pursue coaching further.

In 2014, I began my coach training program at NYU. I had many questions and fears, but I also understood the importance of being open to the experience, as it was unlike anything I had ever done before. This was my chance to embrace the process, reflect on myself, and emerge with a new version of myself, along with new tools, resources, and, most importantly, a new purpose. While I was unsure about what coaching would entail or how it would unfold, I was confident that I would find my way. What I appreciated the most was that it sparked my curiosity rather than filling me with fear or anxiety.

After completing my coach training in August 2014, I was filled with thoughts and questions. Where should I start? How would I find clients? What should I do next? Despite the uncertainty, I felt excitement rather than anxiety! I understood that I couldn't navigate this journey alone, and I was grateful I realized that early on. I highly recommend seeking help whenever you can.

After completing my coach training and beginning to build my business, I joined the International Coaching Federation (ICF) New York City Chapter. I made an effort to meet as many coaches as possible and continued to learn extensively about the industry. I volunteered at events and contributed wherever I could. This involvement was crucial for me, as it provided a way to engage and feel part of something larger. This is the "community" I refer to; it became my anchor.

In 2017, I joined the Board of Directors as the Director of Professional Development for the chapter. This opportunity was exactly what I needed to advance my coaching career. Volunteering in this role introduced me to thought leaders in the coaching field and allowed me to connect with coaches from various backgrounds and training programs. This experience gave me a sense of purpose and direction, ultimately helping me become a better coach. As I grew in this position, I was approached by two board members who encouraged me to consider becoming the next president of the chapter.

I was stunned. Of course, I was honored to be asked, but reality quickly set in. I had so many thoughts and questions that needed to be addressed before making a decision. I had only been coaching for a short time—who would take me seriously? Did I have enough credibility in this field? I didn't know enough people in the chapter or the coaching community. I also lacked a deep understanding of the International Coach Federation (ICF) and how I could learn everything necessary to take on this role. Most importantly, I was seriously concerned about how I would prioritize my clients while building my coaching business, as I knew this position would require a significant amount of my time.

I'll be honest: I was doing a great job of convincing myself that I wasn't qualified or ready for this opportunity, making every excuse to turn it down. I was fully prepared to decline when, one day, during a Zoom call with the two people who had approached me about the presidency, something shifted within me. Without any hesitation, I said yes.

This was the best "yes" I have ever expressed—the best decision and the most challenging undertaking of my career. It would have been unwise to pass on this opportunity early in my coaching journey. The people I would meet, the learning opportunities, and the exposure to the industry were invaluable. Truly, it was the best decision I could have made.

Serving in this role came with its challenges and was often intimidating. There were many moments when I felt overwhelmed and doubted my fit for the board. I was used to jumping in and getting things done myself, but now I had to trust those around me, lead them, and believe that tasks would be accomplished. I was incredibly grateful to be surrounded by amazing people who supported me and ensured that I wouldn't fall or fail, offering help both when I asked for it and when I didn't realize I needed it. This community uplifted me, allowed me to chart a path for growth, and encouraged my curiosity while helping me stay true to myself.

I served on the ICF board for seven years, concluding my term at the end of 2023. It was an incredible experience that helped me discover my identity as a leader and highlighted the importance of community. I know I became a better coach because of the people I was surrounded by and those I met during my time on the board.

As a coach, I learned to ask valuable questions, contribute to building a supportive community, and invest in meaningful conversations. I witnessed how these connections opened doors to new opportunities. The past seven years have been an ongoing journey of learning. As clichéd as it may sound, this experience gave me wings and the ability to reimagine my life in ways I never thought possible.

Being a coach has been an extraordinary experience, but I can't ignore the other important aspects of my life. My identity is not solely defined by my career, and it took me a long time to come to this realization. My journey has involved much more than just becoming a coach and changing careers; it encompasses the entirety of who I am. There have been defining moments along the way, each contributing to who I've become today. Most importantly, I have rewritten my old story and moved on, as I have outgrown my previous self.

I am now telling a new story about myself. My old narrative served its purpose and helped me reach where I needed to be at the time, but this new narrative is opening up fresh opportunities, perspectives, realizations, and "ah hah" moments. I have encountered experiences I never imagined and have undertaken challenges that pushed me well outside my comfort zone. In the past, I was often afraid to take chances and tended to avoid risks. I would automatically say "no" or talk myself out of new or different opportunities. However, I have changed. Now, I pause before making decisions, consider things in ways I never did before, and view my life through a new perspective. I am asking myself better questions and learning to trust myself and my choices.

We all experience moments of self-doubt and impostor syndrome, but it's important to focus on how we respond during those times. It's about moving through the feelings and changing the narrative that keeps us stuck. I've become more resilient and have learned to believe in myself and my self-worth, which has given me newfound confidence. Most importantly, I've learned to appreciate who I am. I no longer dwell on the past, as I know I can't change it. Instead, I view it as an opportunity for growth and learning.

I had to learn to believe in myself, and through that journey, I have become stronger. The person I am on the inside finally aligns with the person I show to the outside world. I've embraced new experiences and committed to my life each day, taking chances on myself. More importantly, I have never felt so seen before.

I must acknowledge that I didn't achieve this growth alone. Asking for help has always been challenging for me, but I did it. I've worked hard through therapy, staying true to who I am, being vulnerable, open to exploration, and giving myself permission to be the person I want to be—not just who I think I have to be.

There have been bumps and bruises along the way, but that is life. Relationships have evolved, and people have come in and out of my life. I know I have changed and grown in all aspects of my life: emotionally, physically, mentally, personally, and professionally. Yet, at the end of the day, I am still here.

I have created a wonderful space to learn, be inspired, contribute, and connect. I always knew this version of me existed, but I didn't know how to access it because I was in my own way and wasn't ready to receive it. However, that has all changed. Here are some things that I know to be true:

- I am now engaged in a never-ending self-development journey, for which I am so thankful.
- Self-awareness has enabled me to become more authentic and has allowed me to embrace my vulnerabilities and emotions in a new way.
- I have learned how to affirm my choices and not spend time justifying them but focusing on reconciling them.
- I have a different kind of confidence than I have ever had.
- I express and support my opinions more easily and often. It's still a work in progress, and I will always work on this.
- I am more in touch with my world and have set much better and clearer boundaries.
- I still suck at dating but not hiding, and I am open to meeting a great guy—I know he's out there.
- I show up every day for my life and am completely present.
- My relationships are more profound, and I have deeper connections with people.

A significant part of this story revolves around my journey of personal growth, self-discovery, and reflection on how I arrived at this point in my life and where I want to go next. What stands out most about this journey is how I confronted my fears and took on an endeavor I had never envisioned for myself: writing a book. This was never something I had planned or considered as part of my work.

Why am I sharing this? I wanted to overcome the self-doubt I had about myself, particularly regarding something I had been judged for in the past. Writing was a monumental fear for me, and I aimed to redefine that fear. I needed to give writing a new meaning because my previous associations with it were rooted in anxiety and vulnerability.

In my senior year of high school, I was diagnosed with a learning disability after years of struggle. This disability affected my test-taking and writing abilities. I chose to attend Westminster College specifically because it had an outstanding program for students with learning disabilities. There, I was able to take tests without a time limit and received additional help with writing papers. I was fortunate to receive incredible support from my professors and a fantastic advisor who guided me throughout those four years.

There's something I must mention because it still strikes me as funny: I am a great note-taker. At the end of each semester, my advisor would always ask for my notes from each of my classes to help his other students. I found this ironic because here I was in a learning disabilities program, yet I was able to assist other students who were struggling as well.

I've carried a fear of writing with me for so long, which has influenced every job I've ever had. I worried that I would be exposed and judged for my abilities. In my last job, before becoming a coach, my boss was highly critical of my writing. He was aware of my disability, but I still felt ashamed. He even required me to take a business writing class, and ironically, I earned an A in that class.

When someone is struggling, the last thing they need is to feel belittled, flawed, or ashamed. Thankfully, there are now better tools and resources available to support individuals with disabilities, as well as greater awareness and understanding. I am grateful that I have learned to extend grace and kindness to myself.

Here's the interesting twist in my journey. Since becoming a coach, I have written chapters for two coaching books. I was also asked to write a book review for a peer, which was included in one of the books, and I was invited to write the foreword for another book. These experiences have been transformative for me.

When I wrote my first chapter, I was so nervous that they would realize I wasn't a good writer and reject it. Luckily, that didn't happen. The biggest surprise came years ago at a work event when someone approached me holding one of the books I had contributed to and asked me to sign her copy. She told me that my chapter had the most significant impact on her of all the chapters in the book. I often struggle with accepting compliments, so I turned red and felt embarrassed. Naturally, I doubted her words, as I tend to tell myself that I am not a writer and that my writing has been criticized in the past.

Being asked to contribute to someone's book was a huge honor. It's amazing how fear and the stories we tell ourselves can stop us in our tracks, paralyze us, and create a narrative that makes us feel unworthy. I often wondered, "Why would someone pick me to contribute to these books?" My first reaction was to decline these opportunities, but I'm so glad I didn't.

These experiences gave me the confidence and courage to write my own book. I had to overcome the belief that I had to do this alone and that I wouldn't get the support I needed or have all the necessary tools and resources. Writing this book turned out to be the scariest, most challenging, and greatest thing I have ever done.

I was fully committed to this project, not just because I wanted to honor the people I interviewed and share their stories, but because it pushed me beyond my comfort zone. It challenged me to pursue something I was passionate about, despite the fear that accompanied it. My new narrative is that I can actually call myself an "author." Never in my wildest dreams would I have used that word to describe myself. I transformed something that felt so fearful into something that became fearless.

I transformed my understanding and definition of fear, and that shift changed everything for me. Naturally, I had fears about moving to New York in 2004 for a job, concerns when I was laid off and had to figure out my next steps, anxieties about going to therapy, and worries when I started my coaching business. However, writing this book brought a different kind of fear. This fear was deeply rooted in me and affected my life in ways I didn't fully realize or want to acknowledge. I have learned to ask myself, "What would I do if I weren't scared?" I believe this is an important question we need to ask ourselves repeatedly, not just once.

Throughout this experience, I have learned that many aspects of life are beyond our control. However, we can control what we focus on, how we react, and where we direct our attention. Being mindful and conscious of these choices is a daily practice that has a significant impact on the quality of our lives. I am grateful that this is a lifelong practice, as it enriches our lives and enhances how we show up for ourselves and others.

My best advice is to jump in, get your feet wet, be curious, and seize opportunities. Say "yes" more often. Trust yourself and the process. You never know what will happen along the way or where the path may lead you. In the journey, you can discover and embrace your true self, acknowledging your strengths, weaknesses, and flaws. The woman I am now is completely different from who I was at the beginning of this book. When I look in the mirror, I smile at the person I see. I received a tremendous gift the day I was laid off, and its impact continues to shape my life. I am excited to see what's next. While I am still finding my way, I know that it only gets better from here.

Take off your armor; dare to be vulnerable,
dare to unwrap yourself, and dare yourself to
be yourself.
—*Maria Shriver*

CONCLUSION

Just because the book has ended doesn't mean our conversations, actions, or voices should stop. We must carry this forward to create the change and compassionate community needed to address layoffs, rethink how we work, redefine our identities, and improve the language we use in our discussions. I hope I have planted a seed of curiosity in you, and that this will inspire movement and progress moving forward. We all know it's much easier to talk about what we need to do and change than to take action. However, that doesn't mean we can't make it happen.

I am committed to continuing this work. I will continue to discuss these important topics, share more stories, support you, and provide the tools and resources you need to help yourself and others. I'm excited to announce that there will be a second book to build on what I've started! I don't want to stop here. We know from the headlines we read, from people we know who have been and will be laid off, and from our own experiences that layoffs will continue to occur. There is still so much more to be done.

Don't stop the work you have hopefully been doing while reading this book. Continue the conversations and remain curious and committed to yourself and others who are going through similar experiences. Share your copy of the book, buy a copy for someone who could benefit from it, or at least tell others about it. Please continue with the exercises and resources I've shared with you.

If you work in a company facing layoffs, share this book with those involved in the decision-making process, those conducting the layoffs, those being laid off, or those remaining at the company. You never know who might benefit from a single story, exercise, or question posed in this book.

Remember, even though we have not met, we share a connection. We are now part of a community, and we don't have to face our challenges alone. Our shared experiences mean we don't have to figure everything out on our own. Connect with one another, engage in meaningful conversations, listen, support each other, trust yourself, and believe in who you are. You will be okay; in fact, you are okay.

Thank you for embarking on this journey with me. I appreciate your willingness to open yourself up, be open-minded, and truly reflect on the tough questions about your life. Thank you for taking the time to be vulnerable and transparent about who you are, for sitting with your emotions, processing your experiences, and taking the leap to navigate your transition and transformation. It's important to see where this journey takes you. We have all faced devastating moments throughout our lives, and how we respond to those moments matters—not just to those around us, but most importantly, to ourselves.

Thank you for choosing to read this book. There's a reason you picked it up, and I appreciate that. You may want to explore and acknowledge the experience of being laid off. My call to action is to encourage you to give yourself the grace and kindness you deserve during this time.

Allow yourself to see where this book takes you and to create a path filled with happiness, authenticity, and compassion for yourself. If you discover someone in your life who might benefit from reading this, please share it with them. I hope this book sparks discussions, gives people a voice, and helps change the perception surrounding layoffs. My wish is for this to be a book you feel compelled to share, knowing it can offer support and guidance to others, just as it strives to help you.

Please let me know if there's anything I can help you with, whether it be questions you have, stories you'd like to share, or anything else.

www.amybloustinecoaching.com

APPENDICES

Appendix 1: Connecting Everything

We have covered a lot of material up to this point. I hope something has resonated with you from the interviews you've read, the questions presented throughout the book, and the various perspectives I've shared about being laid off and its impact on those affected. We can always delve deeper into these topics, and much more can be discussed, but this is an excellent time to connect the dots. We know we need to change how we discuss being laid off, reframe our perceptions of its meaning, and eliminate the shame, guilt, and judgment associated with it. We have recognized that companies need to improve their approach to compassionate layoffs and have explored how to move forward from this experience. If we want to change the conversation on this issue, we must begin discussing it much sooner rather than waiting until it affects us.

Many of us got our first jobs in high school, marking our introduction to the workforce. Some of us may have faced termination from those early positions. It's not just about discussing this with our kids; it's also about what we're teaching them about the workforce. What are we conveying regarding having a job, the possibility of being fired or laid off, and how to cope if it occurs? I held various jobs during high school, from babysitting and nannying to working in retail and waiting tables. Fortunately, I was never laid off or fired from any of them. I also don't recall anyone discussing the possibility of being fired and what that could involve with me.

If this is the case and we are starting to work at a young age, we need to incorporate into the conversation, as part of "career-ing," the distinct possibility that one may be laid off or fired, especially in today's world of layoffs. Let's discuss this sooner rather than later to minimize some of the collateral damage that comes with its impact. By initiating these conversations early, we can help someone manage expectations and possibly soften the blow if or when something like this occurs.

This bonus chapter will discuss how we begin to encounter layoffs and firings even before starting our careers, and when we should have "the talk." We will explore the valuable lessons learned from being laid off and, ultimately, how to make sense of it all. While we could have addressed these topics at the begin-ning of the book, it is now time to conclude with the actions we can take, when to start, how you can get involved—even if you have never experienced this situation—and how we can create and nurture a compassionate community and culture around layoffs that fosters empathy, support, understanding, and growth at any age.

EARLY CONVERSATIONS

When did you get your first job? What did that job mean to you? What did your parents tell you about working? Did your parents encourage you to get a job for spending money? Was it about the importance of having a job, being responsible, accountable, making your own money, and learning to save it? Were you told that working at a young age builds character and prepares you for the future if you understand its significance early? I had to work in high school; I didn't have a choice, and I am so thankful for that.

For many, though not all, who began working in high school, the meaning of work was different from what it signifies to us now. We focus on our careers today, but it was a completely different concept back then. It revolved around opportunities to try new things, gain independence, understand the value of money, earn and save, gain exposure to the real world, build confidence, and learn about potential careers. And let's be honest, it was a valuable addition to our college applications. Whatever it may be, there are significant benefits. If there is an opportunity to set someone up for success at a young age, we need to discuss all aspects: getting the job, doing the job, keeping the job, quitting a job, and the possibility of being fired. All of this is part of the employee lifecycle.

Let's start this early and build on the conversation. Think about your first job and what it represented. Did your parents encourage you to get a job, or was it something you wanted to do? What did you learn about working at such a young age? If you have kids old enough to get a job, what kinds of conversations are you having with them? Even if it's just babysitting or mowing someone's lawn, it is still work and part of having a job. I looked up the definition of a job, and it couldn't be simpler: "A task or piece of work, especially one that is paid." When you think about it, children start working very early. For example, if you give them an allowance for tasks or chores they complete, that's where it begins. If that's the case, let's ensure we use the correct language when discussing getting a job and start these conversations early. Think of it this way: they are building a framework for understanding what it means to work and have a job, which gives them a better chance to manage expectations and themselves should a layoff occur.

WHEN SHOULD WE HAVE THE TALK ... ABOUT BEING LAID OFF OR FIRED?

We have established that having a job at an early age lays the foundation for our expectations as we grow older, continue working, and build a career. Now, we need to prepare for how and when to discuss being laid off or fired. Throughout the book, we have explored in depth the events and impacts associated with such occurrences. Still, we need to find ways to prepare ourselves or at least understand this reality from a different perspective. We cannot erase the devastation of being laid off and its life-changing effects, but what if we cushioned the blow by introducing the concept and the reality that layoffs can and will occur in our careers in various forms?

If you really think about it, the first opportunity we begin experiencing related to having a job and the possibility of being laid off comes during middle and high school. This can actually start when you try out for a sports team, chorus, a school play, or cheerleading, to name just a few. This is essentially a version of an interview where you have to "try out" for any of these. There is a chance you won't get it, or you might be cut from a sports team. This is when we are introduced to what this process looks like. So, if that's the case, how are we preparing for this? What are you teaching your children during this time, and what is the learning opportunity here?

The second opportunity lies in career development during our college years. We start by selecting a major, and then the reality of securing a job becomes apparent as graduation approaches. We strive to create a career plan, learn how to secure a job, maintain it, and advance our careers. As parents, you also work to help them navigate the job search process, offering advice based on your experiences at that age. However, the world has changed since you were searching for a job as a new graduate. For new graduates, the focus is on cultivating a strong work ethic, understanding the process of learning a new trade, developing skills, gaining early experience, and, most importantly, discovering interests that will shape their career paths and portfolios. Many questions arise and are answered through this work experience, leading to positive outcomes that should occur naturally. They learn about the value of money, earning a salary and benefits, building relationships, discovering their lifestyle preferences, and realizing what they want, as well as what they can and cannot afford. Job satisfaction is influenced by the impact of the role and what they enjoy and learn, among other factors.

But where and when is anyone discussing the true arc or lifecycle of an employee and work—the reality that someone can be laid off or fired, what the layoff landscape looks like today, and how it has impacted the workforce? It doesn't seem that conversations about what to do if a layoff occurs, how to prepare oneself, and how to navigate through it are taking place. Again, your job-search experience at that age looked very different, and various factors have come into play now. They also don't need you to organize their job search.

So what should we discuss and explain to our kids about the work experience from when they get their first job, graduate, and build their career portfolio, or "careering?" Your goal is to have an open and honest conversation with them. You can't provide them with a map or guarantees, but you can encourage them, be transparent, and support them. With your support and the career plan they are developing in college, along with this conversation, they have a better chance of being set up for success and managing their expectations.

To effectively guide your college-aged child(ren) through the job search process, encourage open communication, assist them in identifying their interests and skills, and provide resources and support without overstepping. Emphasize that the job search is a learning experience and that they are not expected to have all the answers right away.

Here's a more detailed approach:

1. **Initiate Open Communication:**

    a. **Start Early:** Don't wait until graduation to start discussing the job search. Initiate conversations early in their college journey to allow plenty of time for planning and preparation.

    b. **Create a Safe Space:** Encourage your child to feel comfortable sharing their anxieties, questions, and concerns about the job search.

    c. **Empathy and Understanding:** Be aware of their feelings and recognize the potential frustrations of the job search.

d. **Ask Questions:** Instead of lecturing, pose open-ended questions regarding their career goals, interests, and what they seek in a job.

e. **Encourage Reflection:** Help them think about their skills, strengths, and experiences, and how these could connect to different career paths.

2. **Help Them Identify Career Interests and Skills:**

a. **Encourage them to explore various career fields and industries**: This can occur through research, informational interviews, and job shadowing opportunities.

b. **Connect Interests to Careers:** Help them see how their passions and strengths might translate into potential career paths.

c. **Identify Transferable Skills:** Assist them in recognizing the skills they have acquired through coursework, extracurricular activities, and volunteer work that are beneficial to employers.

d. **Make Use of College Resources:** Remind them of the career services and resources available at their college, including career fairs, resume workshops, and networking events.

3. **Provide Support and Resources:**

a. **Connect with Others:** Introduce them to your professional network and motivate them to establish their own connections.

b. **Offer Financial Assistance:** If necessary and if you can, provide financial assistance to help them manage the expenses of internships, travel, or other job search costs.

c. **Encourage Realistic Expectations:** Help them understand the competitive nature of the job market and the importance of persistence and networking.

d. **Celebrate Small Victories:** Recognize their efforts and achievements during the job search process, even if they don't secure their dream job right away.

4. **Avoid Overstepping or Imposing Your Own Aspirations:**

a. **Respect Their Autonomy:** Let your child make career choices, even if they don't align with your expectations.

b. **Don't Pressure Them:** Avoid making them feel as though they need to determine their career path right away.

c. **Emphasize Learning and Growth:** Present the job search as a chance for learning and personal development, rather than merely a means to an end.

d. **Be patient and supportive:** The job search process can be difficult, so remain patient, understanding, and supportive throughout.

Additionally, if you've been laid off or fired, you can discuss your experiences, the emotions involved, and the impact it had on you. Anything that can enhance this conversation is valuable. You can share your wisdom, insights, and advice with your children and others. I interviewed individuals from all generations for this book and gained significant insights about being laid off as a Millennial, GenX, or Boomer all with various emotions, experiences, and perspectives. Ultimately, this is about how we approach this topic, how we normalize it and create a safe space where it is accepted without shame, guilt, or judgment, recognizing that this is simply part of being an adult, having a job, and building a career.

We need to recognize that we might assume someone entering the workforce after college can't handle this kind of conversation, but they can. Just because it may be difficult for you to discuss this topic doesn't mean it shouldn't happen. This is exactly why we should engage in these conversations. I wish someone had talked to me about what it means to be let go from an organization, because perhaps I could have managed my expectations better and it might have lessened the blow. We never know how we will respond when such an event occurs, but I would prefer to be somewhat prepared for the possibility, to have some information, and then deal with it rather than be blindsided.

Another opportunity that is quite apparent yet often overlooked in many companies is discussing layoffs during the onboarding or hiring process to manage expectations. This may seem counterintuitive since the person is being hired for a role, and nobody wants to think about losing their job. This isn't meant to instill fear, but given the landscape of layoffs that have occurred—especially during and after the pandemic—this conversation should be essential, particularly for those in sectors significantly affected, such as technology or healthcare. The layoff statistics are alarming, and no sector can guarantee job security. In fact, no industry offers guarantees. So, why shouldn't we address this matter? If discussions about the realities of layoffs happen early on, consider the culture of transparency and trust that it could foster. When there's a lack of openness and shared information, we see the negative effects this can have on employees and the organization. Have we not learned anything from the last five years?

If you have not been laid off or fired, are you clear about what this can look like, what it means, and its impact? Knowing someone who has gone through this or who has had to conduct a layoff is an entirely different experience than when it happens to you directly. Your language might differ, and the conversation might change for the person experiencing it firsthand. We must all be on the same page, speak the same language, and show empathy, compassion, and acceptance.

Therefore, if we want to genuinely prepare those entering the workforce, particularly high school students and graduates of undergraduate and graduate programs, it is essential to have this conversation. This should be a required discussion when considering careers and job opportunities. We need to manage expectations, comprehend the real world, and prepare ourselves as thoroughly as possible. We also have discovered many chances to engage in these conversations and learned how to do so effectively. What are you waiting for?

Appendix 2: Additional Interviews

Below are excerpts from other interviews I conducted that were not included in the book's chapters. I wanted to ensure you heard from everyone I interviewed. They graciously shared their journeys of being laid off, each with a unique experience and story. I believe it's important for you to read about them, as their stories of inspiration, passion, and heart can provide comfort and hope. To read the full interviews, please visit www.amybloustine-coaching.com/from-laid-off-to-liberated for complete interviews.

ANONYMOUS: *TO BE LAID OFF IS NOT THE END . . .*

I hope the stigma of being laid off fades away. That would be a silver lining during a very difficult time for so many people. Being laid off is a journey. To be laid off is not an end; it is the beginning of something else. And even though I ended up back in my business, I've learned so much, and I'm in a completely different kind of selling. Like most hardships (other than dying), you can create something good from it, and you will if you persist and try. You may get something different from what you had before. People who get divorced don't find the woman they married twenty years ago, but they find another companion. They find another way to build a community through love. And I think the same about losing a job. You must have faith that you can create something good from it. It might not be the same, but that's okay. Life is change. And we can make positive changes from these experiences.

BRIAN: *FROM FULL-TIME TO FREELANCE*

I struggled with a poor resilience factor, that ability to navigate challenges, which I've had to do for most of my life. It was difficult to summon that resilience and resourcefulness when I'm not feeling good about myself, especially considering the economic situation at the time which was dire. Ad agencies are undergoing changes, either shifting to more in-house models or evolving into entirely different versions. This trend has been developing for several years, and the industry, in general, is facing significant challenges.

As I worked with my therapist, they reminded me, "You've had jobs, and you've been successful at them. That doesn't change now. It doesn't mean you're suddenly not hirable and your skills have disappeared." My wife even said that when I was trying to find my first job out of school, it was probably the hardest time because I had no experience, contacts, or anything. She asked, "Do you feel like you're back there, like you have no prospects?" It felt easier to focus on the things working against me. To be honest and objective, many things were working against me, but there were also things working for me.

CHRIS: *LETTING THE WORLD KNOW YOU ARE STILL BREATHING HAS REAL VALUE*

I now define myself as a late-career, former executive who transitioned to a staff position in a different industry. I'm still a voracious learner. I'm someone who's better equipped to handle organizational change because the skills acquired through a position of transition are permanent additions to one's skill set. I'm a better communicator. I'm more honest with myself. I will always be a self-doubter, and there will always be an element of self-doubt, but it's easier for me to put it aside now. I'm still very critical, and that's just human nature. That's who we all are.

I embarked on a new career path. The work I'm doing now makes a difference in the world, and I am definitely learning new things. For that self-doubter who has lost a job or is undergoing a career transition, who wants to make a change but says, "I'm later in my career; there's no way I could do something like this," you just need a roadmap to achieve it. You must prove yourself, and you can do it. You can talk about making the change, but you have to take action. Get out of your way, and just do it. You will be thankful that you did.

HOWIE: *IF YOU CAN'T LET GO, YOU CAN'T MOVE FORWARD*

I'm still processing the devastation, the shock, and the loss. After I was laid off, I couldn't sleep for weeks. Each day was filled with self-doubt, and I found myself replaying different moments. Did I do something right? Did I do something wrong? Could I have done it better? When you feel like what you've been doing is a huge part of your identity, and then it gets taken away, I would almost compare it to a divorce. When you invest everything into a marriage and suddenly your spouse says, "I'm out," if you've given your all, that was me. That was who I was. It shouldn't be the same, but I loved my work. I was good at it, enjoyed it, and found a good work-life balance. So, it was devastating for months.

I got laid off in 2022, and every once in a while, I wake up feeling upset about the fact that it happened, even though it's not as bad now. I've done everything I can to compartmentalize this, and I understand there's nothing I can do about it since it was completely out of my hands. The more I thought about it, the more I realized that there was nothing I would have changed. I didn't do anything wrong; it's on them. They created that scenario, and the people who did this are in positions they weren't qualified for. But that is not my problem anymore.

ANONYMOUS: *"FOLLOW YOUR GUT"*

Being comfortable with yourself and the choices you are making is really important. I could apply for a job and go back to doing philanthropy or fundraising. But I keep hearing this voice saying, "do you want to do that?" And my answer is no, I don't want to do that. It comes with age and time, figuring out what comes next, and I don't know what that looks like. But I'm determined to get comfortable with it because it's my one life to live, and I don't want to screw it up.

But what a gift I was given: the freedom to be myself, and not many people have that at this stage or at all. How lucky are we that we can make a choice? I want to enjoy what I'm doing, whatever it may be. My point is, it could be working in a bagel shop or a big company; I don't know. But if you're not enjoying it, it's not good for your health, and it's not good for you mentally. It's not good for your friends, and it's not good for your family. It will catch up with you. It's going to bring you down. Don't stay in a place where you're suffering. I don't know why I stayed at that job for so long. I really don't. I say to you, my friend, enjoy what you're doing. And if you need to earn money, find something that brings you joy to make money. I say that to everybody now.

JV: *"WHAT HAPPENS TODAY DOESN'T HAVE A REFLECTION ON WHAT HAPPENS TOMORROW"*

Don't close doors; don't stereotype yourself. You can have a concept, you can have an idea, you can have your dreams, your hopes, and your wants. Let those be your guidelines, but they aren't rules. And those shouldn't be absolute defining factors. This makes you more interesting and more employable down the line because your view is more open. You're more receptive. At the end of the day, your job doesn't define you. Remember, what happens today doesn't reflect what happens tomorrow.

I have been through other layoffs, but after this one, I learned to trust my instincts more than ever. My past experiences serve as a guiding path for what I'm doing now and where I want to go. My final thought is that there will be elements that can be beneficial and enhance your experience of being laid off while helping you move forward. There will be things you feel strongly about, those you believe are right, that resonate with you, and that you know will ultimately lay the foundation for everything ahead. Trust this, and you will emerge from this experience in a way you, hopefully, never thought possible before.

JUDY: *"TIMING IS EVERYTHING IN LIFE"*

Make sure you have a community. Make sure that people know who you are because people will recommend you if something opens up in another company. If people don't know you, if you're invisible, how can somebody recommend you? And even if it is a crappy job, it's still a job with health benefits. The first message is to start. If you've been laid off, don't wait. Get involved. It doesn't mean you have to be active in everything. If there's a trade group or any group, participate. People will know who you are. The second thing is you have to lean on people you know. You never know who will help you and where this help will come from. People want to help; you don't have to do this alone.

I love what I do and the business I'm in. However, after this experience, I realized that this new job has different priorities than before. I'm fine with leaving at five o'clock. I don't have to make all the tough decisions now because I'm not the head of the department. The person I work for handles all the management challenges.

KARI: *"PROCESS IT AND MOVE ON"*

It is how we show up every day. Are you showing up for the ones you love? Are they showing up? Now that I'm on this new journey, it's about breaking down the wall I built up, the armor I had around me, and being okay. I was a very judgmental human being. It took me many years to stop doing that. I want to talk about the stigma of being laid off and allowing myself to be vulnerable while accepting others' vulnerabilities too, without seeing it as a weakness. It's challenging to do. Who are we to judge?

I know it's about our own survival, especially at the moment. But maybe it's about removing the judgment attached to it. It's about eliminating the stigma of being laid off. It's how we talk about it and view ourselves, and we're taking a big, long, hard look at ourselves now because we're spending a lot more time with ourselves. Everyone has their version of how they show up every day.

KERRIE: *"SOME STORIES DON'T HAVE A CLEAR BEGINNING, MIDDLE, AND END.*

It's difficult for people to talk about being laid off. The more we discuss it, the more we learn from our failures and disappointments. We can't grow without feeling uncomfortable, and we can't change without making mistakes or experiencing ups and downs in our lives. We can't become the people we aspire to be without something happening, without encountering experiences that reveal what we are capable of and how we can survive and cope with difficult situations. We should listen and ask, "How did you get through that, and how are you stronger because of it?" I want to learn from that. I want to see how hard you worked and what motivated you to reach that point. And I also want to do the same for myself.

I'm thinking of all the people I turn to in my life for clear advice, and they're all people who've been fired before and will all talk to me about it. And then I know that they've been through something hard, and they're people I admire. I have that much more respect for them. They're the people who guide me when I'm going through something hard because they've been there and understand it. And if it can happen to them, it can happen to me, and so I think that's important. As far as how to get people to talk about being laid off—we need to talk about it.

KRISTA: *"AGE FIFTY AND LAID OFF. WHAT?"*

Here's what I want to share with you. We often feel like we're in control, but this situation was out of my hands, and it truly threw me for a loop. I'm the one who has the power to leave; I have a say over my job. I have never been laid off, fired, or placed on a performance improvement plan. I was really shocked that this could happen to me. It's an interesting lesson: at any time, everything can be taken away from you for no reason or any reason at all. However, you'll never know. When you receive feedback on why you are being laid off, you can process it differently, find closure, and leave knowing, "Well, it's not anything that I did, and I wasn't let go because of performance or cause. I was let go because of certain circumstances." But I had no information in this situation, so how does one gain closure when you truly don't know why?

It's okay and important to grieve and feel upset, angry, scared, and sad when something like this happens. I felt these emotions needed a timeframe: one day, one week, two weeks, or whatever I needed, and then I let them go. I accepted that I would never know the answer. So, I moved on and focused on the positive.

LISA: *"WHEN ONE DOOR CLOSES, ANOTHER DOOR OPENS"*

Make time for self-reflection and consider what you want to do; what would you do differently in your next job? Life continues after your old company. I truly believe that when one door closes, another one opens. Take time to evaluate yourself, your strengths and weaknesses, what you aspire to do, and what you want to avoid. Limit your time wishing you had acted differently and thinking that it might have saved you because it wouldn't have. I pondered over what I could have done differently at my job to try to save it, but there was no saving it. I was doing my best. I was working as hard as I could. No regrets, but examine closely what you are seeking. Take the time to reflect on it; don't just rush into the next opportunity.

MARGOT: *"BEING LAID OFF WAS A GIFT"*

As a result of this whole experience, I believe it has made me a much more empathetic person. Looking back, I used to think they weren't playing the game correctly when I saw people facing workplace struggles. They just weren't figuring it out; they didn't have the savvy to navigate this frustrating game called work. Right? But now, after being laid off, I feel more sympathetic toward those who are unemployed, underemployed, and searching, including those stuck in challenging situations or even those in seemingly good places but feeling trapped due to commitments, unhappiness, or boredom. This experience has deepened my sympathy for people in difficult work environments. I also understand what it feels like to be the recipient of someone who either openly expresses unkindness about being laid off or inadvertently says something hurtful. I am mindful of that when I communicate with others.

I'm in a much better place because of it. If that hadn't happened, I wouldn't be doing what I'm doing now. Overall, it turned out to be a positive experience. It just felt awful while it was happening. I know it's the same for others, too. When you're deep in those emotions, feeling bad for yourself and overwhelmed by sorrow, I can be empathetic and sympathetic up to a point, but you can't feel those emotions for someone else. You can understand, saying, "Oh, yeah, I know that." You can't make them feel better, but you can reassure them, "It does get better over time. You'll figure things out." Sometimes, I think when you're unemployed or feeling desperate, you attempt things you wouldn't normally do. You become a bit bolder than usual, which can lead to more experimentation. When you have nothing to lose, you put yourself out on a limb, which can be beneficial both professionally and personally.

Appendix 3: Reader Engagement Questions by Chapter

CHAPTER 2: BEING LAID OFF VERSUS BEING FIRED:

- Do you fully understand why you were furloughed, laid off, or fired? If not, how can you obtain that information?
- How will you prioritize your mental health and self-care now?
- Do you have a support system to help you during this time? If so, who are they?
- What tools and resources are available to help you navigate through this time?
- Have you asked for help? How can you ask for help during this time?
- Are you comfortable discussing being laid off or fired? If not, what would help you have this conversation?
- Do you have all the information from your company regarding the layoff? This includes details about the severance package, available benefits, unemployment information, health insurance (COBRA), and any other potential eligibility.

CHAPTER 3: THE IMPACT OF BEING LAID OFF:

- How are you taking care of yourself?
- What have you discovered about yourself since being laid off?
- What advice would you offer to someone who has been laid off?
- Is there anything you wish you had done differently after your layoff?
- How can you prepare and protect yourself if you experience another layoff? What could you do differently? (Hopefully, you won't need this!)
- How can you advocate for yourself and your coworkers before, during, and after a layoff?

CHAPTER 4: THE THREE-STATE RECOVERY PROCESS:

- How do you take care of yourself when feeling overwhelmed, stressed, or anxious?
- How can you ensure you are resting and recovering when necessary?
- Are you aware of the physical and emotional signs that indicate your mind and body need rest and recovery? How do you prioritize these needs?
- Do you see your layoff and this time as an opportunity or a hardship?
- Are you working to recover from your layoff, or are you just learning how to move forward?
- If you have the ability to take a sabbatical, or to

take a break before finding a new job, what type of sabbatical would you like to take?

- What is the best way you can structure a sabbatical to maximize its benefits?

CHAPTER 5: CAN YOU RECOGNIZE BURNOUT IN YOURSELF?

- Can you recognize when you're burned out? Do you know what signs to look for?
- Do you plan to deal with your stress when you feel burned out?
- What does your plan look like?
- Do you know the signs of burnout and stress with your team and co-workers?
- Do you feel equipped to support someone who is experiencing burnout and stress?
- How can you talk to your boss when you feel burned out and stressed?
- What gives you energy, and what depletes your energy?

CHAPTER 6: YOUR TRANSITION AND TRANSFORMATION JOURNEY:

- What kind of person do you want to be, and how do you get there?
- Are you stuck in your old narrative?
- What is your new narrative?
- What change do you want to bring to your life?

- What do you want to make, create, or build in your life?
- What gives you meaning in life?
- What can you do if your limiting beliefs are getting in your way?
- What gives you energy?
- What depletes your energy?
- What has worked well for you?
- What have been your challenges?
- What did you learn about yourself after your transition and transformation journey?

CHAPTER 7: INTROSPECTION IS THE GREATEST GIFT TO YOURSELF

- Have you ever taken a moment for introspection without being prompted by an experience, incident, or traumatic event?
- What value did you find from your introspection journey?
- Have you considered incorporating introspection into a regular lifestyle practice instead of only doing it when something is happening?
- How can you incorporate introspection into a regular practice of mindfulness, wellness, and well-being?
- If you have undergone a journey of introspection, what advice would you offer someone about introspection?

CHAPTER 8: ARE YOU JUST YOUR JOB?

- What percentage of your identity is your career?
- How does your career define who you are?
- What do you talk about outside of work?
- What are your hobbies outside of work, and what activities do you enjoy doing?
- What values and characteristics about yourself are important to you?
- How do you want to redefine your identity and create a new narrative about who you are?
- What version of you do you want other people to see?

CHAPTER 9: "LAID OFF" ARE NOT BAD WORDS

- If someone asks you about your layoff, how do you describe it?
- What do you want people to know about being laid off?
- How can we change the conversation about being laid off?
- How can we remove the shame, guilt, embarrassment, and judgment about being laid off?
- What is your advice to someone who has just been laid off?
- What conversations should we have about layoffs?
- How can companies do better when it comes to layoffs?
- What messaging should companies use during a layoff?

CHAPTER 10: SURVIVOR'S GUILT AFTER LAYOFFS:

- How can you establish boundaries with your current work and any work that may be expected of you after a layoff?
- What type of conversation can you have with your boss or manager to ensure clear expectations?
- What steps would you like to take to protect yourself from another possible round of layoffs at your company?
- Were the laid off employees treated with dignity, respect, sensitivity, and concern?
- Did management give a meaningful explanation for the downsizing? Were they open with you about what was happening?
- What does it look like if you remain in your job after a layoff?
- Are you ready to consider a job search if layoffs occur at your company?

CHAPTER 11: MENTAL HEALTH IN THE WORKPLACE AND BEYOND:

- Are you struggling with mental health issues, and do you know your options or how to seek help?
- Do you know somebody struggling with mental health, and what to do if you see somebody struggling?
- Have you taken an inventory of your mental health? Do you know how to do this?

- Do you know the signs or symptoms of mental health issues? Especially anxiety, depression, stress, substance abuse, and burnout.
- Can you recognize when your mental health is affecting your body (physical self)?
- How do your body and mind respond to stress and burnout?
- What kind of mental health support do you need in the workplace?
- How did your current or previous company engage you in a conversation about mental health and burnout?
- What mental health tools and resources are available to you in your workplace?
- How would you ask your manager/boss or HR for support regarding burnout and your mental health?

ACKNOWLEDGMENTS

Writing this book has been a profound journey of personal and professional growth, one I've undertaken with heartfelt gratitude and a strong sense of responsibility. This book results from many factors: the people who believed in me unwaveringly, even when I doubted myself; those who encouraged me when I was struggling, feeling discouraged, and wanting to give up because I feared the book would never be published.

Now, I want to express my gratitude. To everyone who has been part of this journey, your time, support, encouragement, validation, and belief in this passion project have been invaluable. You are the reason this book exists. To my tribe of incredible women who have supported, encouraged, and always looked out for my well-being: you are my true North Star. Thank you for understanding when I had a deadline, for giving me the space to complete the work, and for recognizing my commitment to making this book a reality. I cherish each of you, and I am grateful to have you in my life.

To everyone who sat with me and shared their stories of being laid off: You were vulnerable and courageous, displaying incredible strength. The stories you shared will help others going through the same experience. Your stories made this book real, and I wrote it for you. I wanted you to feel heard and seen. You are pillars of strength and inspiration to me and others. I know you gave hope to those who read this. Thank you for trusting me to tell your story.

To Chris Alvarez: You have been my rock and my sounding board. You offered words of wisdom and sound advice, believing in me every step of the way. You took time from your busy schedule to answer my endless questions, review my work, and help open new perspectives, insights, and "ah" moments. I am blessed and thankful to have you in my life.

To Amy, Craig, and Lucy, my incredible family, from the day I shared with you the path I was on, you have been my cheerleaders. You've given so much love, and I am truly lucky to call you my family.

Thank you to my incredible friends who have stood by me during the craziest and scariest times. For those who cheered me on and supported my dreams and tears, here's to all of you! You know who you are! Thank you to everyone who made me stronger and opened new doors for me to enjoy! I have landed exactly where I always wanted to be. I am truly grateful for each of you. I wouldn't be myself or here without you!

Kimberly Peticolas and Of The Day Press, thank you for believing in me and my vision from the very beginning. Your support helped me overcome my fears and uncertainties. You served as a thoughtful sounding board and fostered a welcoming, collaborative creative process. By taking a chance on me, you made it possible for this book to come to life. I am deeply grateful for your guidance, encouragement, and partnership every step of the way.

ENDNOTES

1 CNN Business, Better.com CEO fires 900 employees over Zoom, by Ramishah Maruf

2 Yildirm, Ece, "2023 layoffs will continue to affect employee morale in 2024, economist says," https://www.cnbc.com/2024/01/03/2023-layoffs-will-continue-to-affect-workers-in-2024-report-says.html, Accessed May 20, 2025.

3 Crawford, Hallie, "Fired vs. Laid Off vs. Furloughed- What's the Difference?" Money.usnews.com, August 11, 2023, https://money.usnews.com/money/blogs/out-side-voices-careers/articles/fired-vs-laid-off-vs-furloughed-whats-the-difference, Accessed October 1, 2023.

4 Contributor, The Wealth Advisor. "Layoffs Soared 98% in 2023 with Employers in Cost-Cutting Mode." The WealthAdvisor, January 4, 2024. https://www.the-wealthadvisor.com/article/layoffs-soared-98-2023-employers-cost-cutting-mode.

5 Whitfill Roeloffs, Mary. "2024 Had Most Job Cuts In 15 Years—With One Exception." Forbes, January 9, 2025. https://www.forbes.com/sites/maryroel-offs/2025/01/09/2024-had-most-job-cuts-in-15-years-with-one-exception/.

6 Challenger, Gray & Christmas. "Job Cuts Rise 5.5% Over Last Year; 38,792 in December 2024." Challenger, Gray & Christmas, Inc. | Outplacement & Career Transitioning Services, January 9, 2025. https://www.challengergray.com/blog/job-cuts-rise-over-last-year-38792-in-december-2024/.

7 Peppercorn, Susan. "Digital Article Stress Management Managing Your Emotions After Being Laid Off." Harvard Business Review, January 17, 2023. https://www.harvardbusiness.org/wp-content/uploads/2023/03/2023_01_managing-your-emotions-after-being-laid-off.pdf.

8 Cohen, Jack. "Everyone Wants To Have An 'Impact' But What The Heck Does That Mean?" Medium.com, February 7, 2019, https://medium.com/the-ascent/every-one-wants-to-have-an-impact-but-what-the-heck-does-that-mean-642e7da0345, Accessed December 1, 2023.

9 "Recovery Definition & Meaning," Merriam-Webster, accessed November 23, 2025, https://www.merriam-webster.com/dictionary/recovery.

10 Perry, Elizabeth, "How to Get Permission for Taking a Sabbatical From Work," Betterup.com, February 24, 2023, https://www.betterup.com/blog/taking-a-sab-batical-from-work, Accessed November 8, 2023.

11 Yang, Nu, "More Employers are Offering Sabbaticals to Prevent Employee Burnout," Worldatwork.org, March 17, 2022, https://worldatwork.org/resources/publications/workspan-daily/more-employers-are-offering-sabbaticals-to-pre-vent-employee-burnout, Accessed November 8, 2023.

12 Ibid.

13 Overton, Jennie, "Employee burnout statistic for 2023," Limeade.com, August 11, 2022, https://www.webmdhealthservices.com/blog, Accessed December 27, 2023.

14 Ibid.

15 Farrugia, JD, "9 crucial employee burnout statistics & trends (2023)," Workforce. com, May 3, 2023, https://workforce.com/news/statistics-on-employee-burnout, Accessed December 27, 2023.

16 Mayo Clinical Staff, "Know the signs of job burnout," Mayoclinic.org, June 5, 2021, https://www.mayoclinic.org/healthy-lifestyle/adult-health/in-depth/burnout, Accessed, December 27, 2023.

17 Feiler, Bruce. *Life is in the Transitions: Mastering Change at Any Age.* New York, NY: Penguin Books, 2020. Pg. 143.

18 Huffington, Arianna, "How to Make the Most of Our Collective Life Transition," LinkedIn.com, July 24, 2020, https://www.linkedin.com/pulse/how-make-most-our-collective-life-transition-arianna-huffington, Accessed December 2, 2023.

19 Rosenberg, Robin S. "Being in Transition." Psychology Today, November 10, 2014. https://www.psychologytoday.com/us/blog/being-in-transition/201411/being-in-transition-1.

20 Cooks-Campbell, Allaya. "Human Transformation: What It Means to Become More You." BetterUp, January 20, 2022. https://www.betterup.com/blog/human-transformation.

21 Hale, Mandy. *The Single Woman–Life, Love, and a Dash of Sass: Embracing Singleness with Confidence.* Peabody, MA: Thomas Nelson, 2013.

22 Nardine, "12 Powerful Quotes from Arianna Huffington's Book "On Becoming Fearless" https://medium.com/@nardineta/12-powerful-quotes-from-arianna-huffingtons-book-on-becoming-fearless-a91bb870c108, Accessed May 21, 2025.

23 Volpe, Allie. "How to Get Over Losing Your Job." Medium, September 26, 2019. https://forge.medium.com/how-to-get-over-losing-your-job-1b6411cd0699.

24 Ibid.

25 Rathore, Shyamli, "How to Emotionally Process a Layoff," Harvard Business Review, February 14, 2023, https://hbr.org/2023/02/how-to-emotionally-process-a-layoff, Accessed, November 19, 2023.

26 Koretz, Janna, "What Happens When Your Career Becomes Your Whole Identity," Harvard Business Review, December 26, 2019, https://hbr.org/2019/12/what-happens-when-your-career-becomes-your-whole-identity, Accessed, July 23, 2023.

27 McGeorge, Donna, "Don't Feel Guilty for Prioritizing Yourself Over Work," Harvard Business Review, November 14, 2022, https://hbr.org/2022/11/dont-feel-guilty-for-prioritizing-yourself-over-work, Accessed, July 23, 2023.

28 Rubens, Aaron, "How to conduct compassionate layoffs & boost morale in their wake," Hrmorning.com, May 3, 2023, https://www.hrmorning.com/articles/compassionate-layoffs, Accessed February 2, 2024.

29 Brown, Brené. *Daring Greatly: How the Courage to Be Vulnerable Transforms the Way We Live, Love, Parent, and Lead.* New York, NY: Avery, 2012.

30 Zacks, Leslie Kleinberg, "Nobody Cares That You Were Fired," Productcoalition. com, December 19, 2019, https://productcoalition.com/nobody-cares-that-you-were-fired-d6d49a3a942b, Accessed February 14, 2024.

31 Murphy, Mark, "Don't Expect Layoff Survivors To Be Grateful (Survivor's Guilt After A Downsizing)," leadershipiq.com, 2008, https://www.leadershipiq.com/blogs/leadershipiq/29062401-dont-expect-layoff-survivors-to-be-grateful, Accessed December 12, 2023.

32 Corrigan, John. "Workplace survivor syndrome can wreak havoc on your business: experts." March 6, 2023. https://www.hcamag.com/us/specialization/employee-engagement/workplace-survivor-syndrome-can-wreak-havoc-on-your-business-experts/438419

33 Davisson, Abby and Strober, Myra H., "You Survived a Layoff. Here's What to Do Next," Harvard Business Review, April 25, 2023, https://hbr.org/2023/04/you-survived-a-layoff-heres-what-to-do-next, Accessed December 13, 2024.

34 Kaplan, Dr. Beth, "The Devastating Impact of Layoffs on Employee Sense of Belonging," LinkedIn, February 26, 2023, https://www.linkedin.com/pulse/devastating-impact-layoffs-employee-sense-belonging-kaplan-ed-d-/, Accessed, December 13, 2023.

35 Robinson, Bryan, "74% Of Employees Report Negative Mental Health At Work" https://www.forbes.com/sites/bryanrobinson/2024/05/21/74-of-employees-report-negative-mental-health-at-work, Accessed May 21, 2025.

36 This is a widely cited statistic that originates from data collected by U.S. government sources, particularly the Substance Abuse and Mental Health Services Administration (SAMHSA) and the National Institute of Mental Health (NIMH)

37 Robinson, Ph.D., Bryan, "Mental Health Related Leaves-Of-Absence Up 300% Since 2017," Forbes.com, August 10, 2024, https://www.forbes.com/sites/bryanrobinson/2024/08/10/mental-health-related-leaves-of-absence-up-300-since-2017, Accessed, December 4, 2024.

38 "Mental Health," The World Health Organization, June 17, 2022, https://www.who.int/news-room/fact-sheets/detail/mental-health-strengthening-our-response, Accessed October 4, 2023.

39 "What is mental health in the workplace?" Hibob.com, https://www.hibob.com/hr-glossary/mental-health-in-the-workplace, Accessed October 4, 2023.

40 Fisher, Jen, "As workforce well-being dips, leaders ask: What will it take to movethe needle?" Deloitte.insights.com, June 20, 2023, Accessed October 4, 2023.

41 Ibid.

42 American Psychological Association, www.apa.org/topics, Accessed October 4, 2023.

43 "Recognizing warning signs of mental health issues in the workplace is important and necessary," Purdue University, October 13, 2021, https://www.purdue.edu/newsroom/purduetoday/releases/2021/Q4/recognizing-warning-signs-of-mental-health-issues-in-the-workplace-important,-necessary.html, Accessed October 4, 2023.

44 "2023 Workforce Mental Health Trends Forecast," Lyrahealth.com, Accessed October 4, 2023.

45 SHRM.org, "As Workplace Mental Health Worsens, Employee Engagement Plummets,"General Dynamics Information Technology, July 4th, 2023, https://www.gdit.com/perspectives/gdit-in-the-news/as-workplace-mental-health-worsens-employee-engagement-plummets, Accessed October 4, 2023.

ABOUT THE AUTHOR

A MY BLOUSTINE has more than twenty-five years of experience in entrepreneurship and non-profit work. In 2014, she founded Amy Bloustine Coaching, which specializes in life and career coaching, layoff coaching and consulting, and time management coaching. Additionally, she has established a non-profit organization, worked for the DEA Educational Foundation, and worked for a national non-profit organization dedicated to reducing teen substance abuse and supporting those affected by addiction.

Amy holds a B.A. in Psychology and a minor in Business from Westminster College. She also has a Masters in Educational Psychology from Texas A&M University. In addition, she is an NYU-certified Life Coach, a GetFive Certified Master Career Coach, and a trained Recovery Coach through CCAR. Furthermore, she served as the director of professional development, president, and past president of the Board of Directors for the NYC International Coaching Federation Chapter from 2017 to 2023.